Praise for *Growing Your Business 1, 2, 3*

"… an easy but incredibly effective way of focusing on important business objectives and the strategies for making them happen … You will not be disappointed with the results you create from using this book."

—Terry Truesdell, President/CEO, National
LTC Network, Overland Park, Kansas

"Dick is a rare individual who not only understands successful business principles, but who also has the unique ability to lead the process and the path to business success. His strategic business planning model works, and the success and prosperity that his companies have achieved over the years are a sound testament to this."

—James F. Scarpone, CFP, CPA, CVA,
Niles, Michigan

"You can't go wrong if you follow his principles."

—Steven P. Stucky, CLU, Chairman and CEO,
S. P. Stucky Company, Inc.,
West Lafayette, Indiana

"An excellent primer to get started in developing strategic planning skills."

—Donald C. Werme, Entrepreneur, President
and CEO (Retired), Kalamazoo, Michigan

"Strategic planning is one of the essential skills that every [entrepreneur] needs to master to achieve success in the business world … well-written and a step-by-step guide to building a successful business plan that will help drive and achieve [your] business objectives."

—Mary Anne Gale, Vice President, Proctor &
Gamble–Asia (Retired),
Mullett Lake, Michigan

"Sanford makes no magical promises for success, instead [he] supplies the tools that, coupled with hard work and passion, promote financial achievement. Small business owners will find this book an invaluable resource for themselves and their [business]."

—Sue Bronson, Cheboygan, Michigan

"Dick Sanford makes strategic planning simple to understand; showing [entrepreneurs] how to think, plan, and execute business plans."

—Tim Blake, President, Land Care
Unlimited, LLC, Litchfield Park, Arizona

GROWING
Your Business
1, 2, 3

GROWING
Your Business
1, 2, 3

The Go-To Manual for Entrepreneurs
Who Want to Expand Their Business

RICHARD B. SANFORD

Sanford Publishing Company, LLC

DISCLAIMER

Growing Your Business 1, 2, 3, was crafted from the personal experiences of the author and is offered as a guide to other entrepreneurs who are seeking growth and expansion for their business enterprises. Readers are free to use or not the Strategic Planning information and Model presented within and are solely responsible for the results obtained.

The author and publisher are not and will not be responsible for any loss, liability, or risk encountered as a result of using the contents of this book.

Sanford Publishing Company, LLC

P. O. Box 66 / Mullet Lake, MI 49761

growyourbusiness123.com

ISBN: 978-0-692-61987-2

Library of Congress Control Number: 2016900649

Printed in the United States of America

For volume discounts inquire at www.growyourbusiness123.com.

Richard B. Sanford is available to train and consult with individuals and groups. To inquire about his availability, please e-mail him at: sanford@growyourbusiness123.com.

Cover and text design by Mary Jo Zazueta (tothepointsolutions.com)

To the continued expansion of
America's entrepreneurial spirit
and the successful small businesses that follow.

CONTENTS

**Every small-business success
is the result of an entrepreneur's thinking.**

**Every small-business failure
is the result of insufficient planning.**

PREFACE

EVERY BUSINESS ORIGINATES WITH A DREAM—AN IDEA—
an entrepreneurial seed. Consider the businesses in
your community. Each one, whether small, midsize,
big, or international in scope, had its start from one person's
vision.

Regardless of what you hear about the demise of America
being a flagship of innovation and creativity, know this: our
country is the world's garden of small business. Every day,
domestic and international businesses that benefit Americans and people throughout the globe are cultivated in the
United States.

Another truth you should know is how difficult it is for
small businesses to survive and grow during the first one
to three years—the period when 80 percent of startups fail.
Since you are reading this book, however, I presume you
don't want to become a part of that statistic.

Congratulations! You are a survivor at heart. You seek
reliable information about how to make your business grow
and prosper. I wrote this book for people like you.

I used the planning tools in this book to grow eleven
small businesses—each a business I founded. Most, but not
all, became Phase 2 businesses and two grew much larger,
with one, the Sanford Insurance Group Inc., a third-party
insurance administration company, generating over $136

million in annual sales revenue. Each business, successful in its own right, shared a common vision: creating ever-increasing sales, income, and profit—or I'd sell it, merge it, or close its doors and move on.

Because of my reputation and track record as a successful entrepreneur, people continue to ask: What was the key to my success? How can they grow their businesses and bottom lines like I did?

In *Growing Your Business 1, 2, 3*, I answer those questions. The information in this book is based on a simplified Strategic Business Planning model I created and used in my businesses. It is a common-sense, easy-to-use, business-management model that worked for all of my enterprises—and it can work for you and yours also!

Is strategic planning something new? Heck no! Strategy has been used since the Dark Ages by military leaders and emperors to win wars, like Alexander the Great; by political leaders to expand their countries' borders and economic power, like England; and even by the founders of the United States of America when creating our great country.

But, if you look for books on how to grow and expand a business by using a Simplified Strategic Business Plan, you won't find any (except for the one in your hands). I know, because I have searched in bookstores and online for many years. You will find books on how to start a business, how to prepare a business plan, and even how to sell a business. These books on the *functions* of business abound i.e., human resources, finance and accounting, sales management, marketing and advertising, etc. but none I found discussed a Simplified Strategic Business Planning model for entrepreneurs to use in managing their business to success.

Additionally, many of the books are written by professors and bigger business leaders with impressive credentials (evidenced by the letters that follow their names), but teaching *about* business is not the same as being an entrepreneur with the experience of running a business. Time spent before students in a lecture hall focusing on a Big Biz approach to succeeding in the small business arena—completely ignoring the real conditions entrepreneurs face—the real job creators and the backbone of our economy—is no substitute for the roll-up-your-sleeves, real-time experiences of the entrepreneurial business world.

Consider for a moment why there is such a drastic failure rate (80 percent) by entrepreneurs in both their initial start-up and first-year phase, and their three- to five-year survival phase. The reason for this is our nation's educational system—which the last time I checked, does not offer Entrepreneurial Management Skills training in high school or college. Students interested in small business are not taught how to make the right decisions that result in success or how to avoid making the wrong business decisions that breed failure.

What is offered in high school and beyond are subjects that describe the *functions* of business.

What are the functions of business? There are seven: Marketing, Sales, Administration, Human Resources, Internet Technology, Manufacturing/Services*, and Finance. These functions are about how to operate a business but not about how to manage a business—which is critical for entrepreneurial success.

Thus, I realized the need for a practical text based on

* Wherever the word *manufacturing* appears, it is also meant to include *services*. Just as some companies sell manufactured products, others specialize in offering services.

my experiences—a Simplified Strategic Business Planning model—a business road map that will guide you and other entrepreneurs toward expansion and continued success.

What is different about *GROWING Your Business 1, 2, 3?*

This book is a result of many years of hands-on entrepreneurial experience and is a straightforward presentation of how a Strategic Business Plan works. Business plans that deal with the functions of business are not *strategic* in nature. A Strategic Business Plan must come first; it is the foundation for every business decision and should be the foundation for every entrepreneurial decision you make. Basing your business plan on the functions of business does not hold your Strategic Business plan accountable for positive results. That is what a Strategic Business Plan does!

In the comfort of your home or office, you can now learn a simple and efficient way to grow your business by using my Strategic Business Planning model, a proven recipe for success that is based on three stages:

THINKING Business
PLANNING Your Business
WORKING Your Business

Visit my website—www.growyourbusiness123.com—to discover the *results* you can expect when using a Strategic Business Plan to make the right business decisions that create ever-increasing sales, income, and profits.

INTRODUCTION

AMERICA'S ENTREPRENEURIAL GARDEN IS A CRITICAL resource for our country's economic survival. Over 70 percent of U.S. job creation comes from successful small businesses—businesses that began with ideas we planted, watched germinate, and hoped to expand and harvest.

Even though most start-up entrepreneurs fail to achieve long-term success, the entrepreneurial garden you have undertaken is a worthy and noble career because YOU ARE DIFFERENT! You are reading this book to acquire knowledge and information that will help you transform how you think about business.

"It is your thinking that decides whether you are going to succeed or fail."

~ Henry Ford

STARTING a BUSINESS IS EASY!—the challenge is learning how to grow your business so it survives beyond the first one to three years. Presumably you understand that the way to pass this benchmark is to increase your sales, income, and profit—which is why you are reading *Growing Your Business, 1, 2, 3.*

But, first a question:

Is the effort to expand your business worth the stress, anxiety, and expense you will need to invest?

If you answered yes, then proceed. If you answered no, stop reading this book and know that if you continue to work by the seat of your pants with unproven and unreliable intuition "guiding" you, your odds of success are slim and your odds of failure are substantial.

First, you need to create a foundation for your business. Just like a house, the strength and longevity of your business depends on the sustainability of its foundation. Every decision you make, every action you take, every project and process begins from a starting point. For entrepreneurs, the starting point is your business mission and purpose. All else follows.

A business mission is **what you want your business to do for you**. In chapter 2, I show you how to create a business mission.

A business purpose is **what your business will do to satisfy the wants and needs of your customers and clients**. In chapter 3, I explain how to create your business purpose.

Whether you are interested in exploiting untapped markets, adding new products and services, or adding new equipment to an existing facility, *Growing Your Business 1, 2, 3* will guide you through the strategic planning process, using informative text, interactive dialogue, and probing questions. These tools "attack" the brain-lock that can prevent entrepreneurs from learning new ways to successfully manage their businesses.

Successful entrepreneurs with passion, creativity, and an

independent spirit know how to start a business but even established enterprises, at some point, reach a plateau where they must reassess the business model that first brought them initial success and ask:

▲ **How do I increase sales of my products and/or services?**

▲ **How do I transfer my business vision and goals to my staff?**

▲ **How do I motivate my employees to make positive results?**

▲ **How can I find lower-cost products and services?**

▲ **How do I expand?**

▲ **How do I find new products?**

▲ **How do I create new services?**

▲ **How do I find new markets?**

▲ **How many employees and managers will I need?**

▲ **What new equipment will be required to support growth?**

▲ **Where and how do I get funding for expansion?**

In this book, I show you how to recognize if you're on the right (or wrong) path and how to correct your business plans and actions to avoid wasting your investment capital and operating funds. I walk you through the three stages of creating a strategic business plan with the goal of increasing your business profits and personal wealth. These stages, coupled with my Strategic Business Planning model, take the guesswork out of managing a business, eliminate mistakes and losses, reduce the odds of failure, and greatly increase your chances of success.

When you use these tools and embrace the philosophy behind *Growing Your Business 1, 2, 3*, you will have more confidence and acquire total control of your business results; while enjoying the pleasure of owning and operating a business—the benefits you expected when you first dreamed of starting a business and becoming an entrepreneur.

"HOLD ON A MOMENT!" you say. "I'm not sure I want to do the necessary reading and thinking and writing to improve my business management methods."

Well, maybe that's because you haven't focused on the other responsibility you have in addition to working your business.

AS AN ENTREPRENEUR, YOU HAVE TWO JOBS!

The first one is doing the *work* of the business. The other is *managing* the business. It is this responsibility of managing the business that is most often overlooked, even ignored, by entrepreneurs, which results in our nation's dismal small-business success rate of 20 percent.

As you read, think, and create your Strategic Business Plan chapter by chapter, write down your answers to questions in the spaces provided on the forms (full-page forms are available to download from www.growyourbusiness123. com). I recommend you use a pencil (with a good eraser) because your plan is a living document. You will make changes along the way until you get it just right, and then it will change again to meet new conditions that always surface in your chosen markets.

When you finish creating and reading your way through

this book, do NOT put your business plan in a desk drawer where it is likely to be forgotten. Your Strategic Business Plan should be in full view, to guide and help you every day as you face and make decisions that will make your business grow. Mine could be found resting on my desk for easy reference throughout the day.

NOTHING HAPPENS until
YOU TAKE THE FIRST STEP!

So, let's begin.

STAGE I

How to THINK
Business

CHAPTER 1

Why You Need a Strategic Business Plan

"Dreams and ideas require planning to become reality."
~ Richard B. Sanford

OST PEOPLE DESCRIBE A SMALL BUSINESS AS A COMPANY with a certain number of employees or a certain level of income. I define a small business as an enterprise that has survived the critical one- to three-year start-up period (the benchmark survival time), has less than 100 employees, and generates profit. Income is not a credible measurement of whether a business is small or large. Many small businesses generate millions of dollars in annual revenue, but at the bottom line, where it counts, show little or no profit. (The same is true for many large businesses.)

Size does not determine success, profits do!

Phase 1 small businesses include startups and companies that elect to remain small; generating a comfortable income and employing few people, often with no additional managers other than the owner and family members.

Phase 2 small businesses have survived the start-up phase and the one- to three-year high-risk period and are now ready and wanting to expand.

Eventually every entrepreneur stands at a fork in the road—a time when he or she must start to rely on others to get positive business results; especially to **grow** the business. Self-reliance, intuition, and instinct are insufficient to grow a business!

Self-reliance is "the act of relying solely upon self for help, aid, answers, etc."

Intuition is "the power of knowing things without conscious reasoning."

Instinct is "the tendency to respond to stimuli without involving reasoning."

At this juncture, it is imperative that you create a plan for the future of your business. Engage your key employees to work with you in creating business objectives. Anyone charged with responsibility for achieving positive results through the action of others, whether boss, owner, partner, vice president, manager, spouse, or key employee, should participate. Encourage input from the employees closest to your customers and suppliers. Many best ideas for new products, new markets, and learning what your prospects/customers "want' come from these sources—but always remember: you are the boss. What is included in your Strategic Business Plan is ultimately your decision.

A Strategic Business Plan is comprised of words, sentences, and paragraphs that describe actions to take; whereas traditional business plans consist mainly of numbers with a focus on pro-forma financial statements, sales projections, cash flow, etc.

A Strategic Business Plan is superior to a traditional business plan.

A Strategic Business Plan is superior to a traditional business plan because it demands the entrepreneur visualize and record, in detail, the mission, purpose, and objectives for the business; followed by what strategic actions are necessary to achieve those goals. In other words, basing business decisions on your Strategic Business Plan will greatly enhance your odds of achieving positive results rather than basing business decisions on intuition, instinct, and guesswork— or the ideas and suggestions from well-meaning people who have no personal financial risk in the success or failure of your business.

A Strategic Business Plan is a written, uncomplicated, focused plan with clear steps that outline how to accomplish your business goals.

A traditional business plan is usually prepared with input from accountants who get information from the entrepreneur and his lenders and attorneys—the people who provide a financial loan to fund or expand the enterprise. A traditional business plan is expressed in terms of numbers—sales, income, and expenses. These business plans are typically rooted in a subset of *assumptions* decided by the entrepreneur. An assumption is a "best guess" made by the entrepreneur when envisioning what future products, sales, markets, etc. might look like. Oftentimes things go wrong because the assumptions are wrong.

To avoid falling prey to faulty assumptions that lead a business in the wrong direction (and dupe the entrepreneur into believing positive results will occur even though careful research says differently) thoughtful entrepreneurs create a Strategic Business Plan and use it to gain funding. Assumptions based on a carefully constructed Strategic Business Plan are more accurate and dependable and more likely to generate successful funding results.

Unfortunately, many entrepreneurs lack an understanding of how to *think* before planning.

It is critical you understand that business activities follow a natural progression of functions, namely: What? Why? Want? How? Who? When?

To grow a business, you must be able to answer the following questions:

- ▲ **WHAT do you want to do?** (YOUR MISSION)

- ▲ **WHY do you want to do it?** (YOUR PURPOSE)

- ▲ **What do you WANT to achieve?** (OBJECTIVES)

- ▲ **HOW will you make it happen?** (STRATEGIES)

- ▲ **WHO will do it?** (ACTION PLAN)

- ▲ **WHEN will it be done?** (MANAGING FOR POSITIVE RESULTS)

The heart and soul of any small business—that quality of mind that enables entrepreneurs to stand resolute in the face of opposition and competition, is a Strategic Business Plan—a framework that outlines how to "THINK" first, then "PLAN," followed by "ACTIONs" in pursuit of your business mission. In other words, how to make business decisions that result in positive outcomes.

You are in the driver's seat. Using the proven tools in this book will move your business forward. Strategic business planning offers you:

1. A destination-focused journey, including detailed plans for the path your business should follow.

2. The opportunity to identify the challenges you, as an owner, must overcome.

3. Ample "refueling" stops along the way to review action plans for key players, including managers and employees.

4. Specific directions to help you increase sales, income, and profits.

5. A timetable for arriving at your business destination.

This will be no ordinary road trip.

As a savvy entrepreneur, you already know to expect a bumpy ride filled with bends and occasional dead ends—even a flat tire or two. You've been on this road long enough to recognize the competitive economic climate that colors today's entrepreneurial landscape. You are on your own, but not *alone*—not if you incorporate the tools in this book.

When you use the methods in this book, you will be able to confidently look ahead to what is next because you will want to accelerate growth utilizing your own intellectual capital and the human capital available through specific key employees—the ones closest to your customers and markets.

As entrepreneurs, we are risk takers and gamblers by nature—BUT we also base decisions on facts and known information, not guesswork or unproven assumptions that cost you money!

As a business owner, you want more than a path to success. You want good odds. So you might ask, "How do I increase my chances to successfully reach my sales, income, and profit goals?" The answer: by creating a Strategic Business Plan using current and accurate market data gleaned from your Research and Development efforts.

Always remember, you are in control. You will influence your success by following the blueprint provided in this book. Now, get behind the wheel and fasten your seatbelt. It is time to move your business forward to a more successful and profitable future.

After completing the exercises in *Growing Your Business 1, 2, 3* you will have an action plan with clearly defined objectives and strategies, outlining the steps you will take to expand your business. The result: your confidence will soar *and* your company will grow!

Sound easy? It is—but you will have to work at it.

Now, let's get started. The first step is to create your business mission.

CHAPTER 2

Creating a Business Mission

"The beginning is the most important part of the work."

~ Plato

THE FIRST ELEMENT OF A STRATEGIC BUSINESS PLAN IS THE mission. *Mission?* Hmm, is that a goal, a vision, or possibly a military combat exercise? What exactly is it? Well, most entrepreneurs base their business mission and purpose on their vision for the business. Although some entrepreneurs use the word *goal* to describe the mission of their business, I define *mission* as "the entrepreneur's reason for starting and owning a business."

Objectives and strategies are goals and certainly they play a part when developing a plan, but mission encompasses more. You, as an entrepreneur, have a mission; in fact, every business owner has a mission, whether it is in writing, orally expressed, or in thought only.

Perhaps you are an investor. If so, you've seen annual reports sent out to shareholders. Sure, they look wordy and boring, but there is a story that unfolds in their pages, and the story often portends a great ending, although sometimes not. Much depends on the numbers and also on where a firm is ultimately headed—the direction is set at the beginning of every annual report with a few words about the company's mission.

Read several annual reports and you will find that good mission statements usually match with continuously successful companies, while poorly crafted proclamations tend to trend with less stellar performances. Check out the following examples.

"Oh" Missions and Other Mishaps

Example 1: Barnes and Noble (B&N), a leading bookseller in the United States, reported in its *1998 Annual Report*: "Our Mission: bring books and bookstores into the mainstream of American life."[1] Here is what they missed: There was no mention of increasing company income and profits or shareholder wealth; both necessary for the company to prosper and succeed. Between 1998 and 2010, a major change in the consumer market occurred. Consumers suddenly had new options for obtaining reading material, whether for purposes of entertainment or information gathering. Then on August 19, 2010, *Yahoo! News* carried this message: "Barnes & Noble (B&N) declined an offer to sell the company."

Why was B&N looking to sell its business? Sales were declining, in part it seems because their business model, *which focused on selling books rather than on selling reading enjoyment and a convenient learning experience*, did not keep pace with changing technology. Amazon had expanded its

---

1. Barnes & Noble, *1998 Annual Report* (New York: Barnes & Noble, 1998), pg. 6.

reach by introducing the Kindle, and then the Sony Reader debuted, making it easier for customers to instantly download books, both new releases and classics, at much lower costs. B&N did not keep pace with its competitors, and both its hardcover and paperback book sales started to dry up.

In its *2008 Annual Report*, B&N reported lower sales and income, lower profits of 29.1% and lower per share prices (lower shareholder wealth.) Additionally, instead of a focus on increasing sales, income, and profit, the chairman touted "curling up with a good book on the sofa" as a major goal.[2] I suspect the book he referred to was not a new, lower cost, instantly delivered e-book. In fact, the B&N Nook did not debut until December 2009.

When a mission statement veers off course from the primary goal of ever-increasing sales, income, and profit, bad things follow. B&N should have answered with "What's new? What technological advances are available that will enable us to continue selling books profitably and create more income for the business and wealth for the shareholders?" The answer should have been incorporated into its mission statement, but it doesn't appear that it was.

Furthermore, B&N failed to partner the answer with a marketing strategy. Had they done so, perhaps B&N would have led and not followed the e-book craze.

> **Example 2:** A small Midwest bank holding company's 2004 Annual Report stated: "Mission: What We Want To Be … Irwin Financials mission is to be the best financial services company through ethics and excellence, today and tomorrow."[3]

The mission published in Irwin Financial's annual report

---

2. Barnes & Noble, *2008 Annual Report* (New York: Barnes & Noble, 2008), pg. 3-6.
3. *Irwin Financial Corporation 2004 Annual Report* (Columbus: Irwin Financial, 2004), pg. 20.

did not focus on how to generate ever-increasing sales, income, and profit to survive in the marketplace. It talked "tall" but didn't explain how to "climb the wall." The result: investors lost hundreds of millions of dollars and the company folded in 2009.

(If you invest in any business as a shareholder or lender, read the annual reports because it is imperative that you understand the stated mission of the business so you can evaluate if it is focused on a mission that makes sense.)

The ONLY legitimate and appropriate mission of a for-profit business is: CREATE EVER-INCREASING SALES, INCOME, AND PROFIT FOR THE COMPANY.

Over the years, I have heard much ranting and raving against the above mission statement. Some condemn it, calling it greedy, insensitive, and inappropriate for society. Well, does a business need to maintain its income and profit to continue in business? Do you think it is possible to have a successful business future with *declining* customers, sales, income, and profit?

A company that is losing money has no wealth to share with employees, managers, and owners; and without a fast and effective turnaround it will implode. Then POOF! No more income, no more jobs, and the owner's investments and the entrepreneur's dreams are gone.

Ever-increasing income and profits are the *only* way to increase employee wages, job opportunities, bonuses, company perks, pensions, and profit-sharing plans—and it doesn't stop there. Society benefits and local community coffers grow, along with state and federal tax revenues. As consumers confidently spend their cash earned by working at firms with clear-cut missions and consistent track records, sales-tax revenue increases and property assessments climb in tow with personal net worth. On the federal side, real net job expansion and income growth make for higher income-tax revenues, and Medicare and Medicaid, and Social Security tax receipts—all needed to fund these government-promised programs.

When the business sector thrives, there is more room for philanthropic pursuits, in the form of support for the arts, sciences, education, and other goodwill.

Companies can only make charitable contributions when they have "excess" earnings, which only happens by achieving ever-increasing sales, income, and profit.

Indeed, where do the naysayers of ever-increasing sales, income, and profit believe employee and community benefits come from? The government? Competitors? Some other source? WRONG!

The financial health of a business, its employees, its owners, and the surrounding community and beyond, comes from the continued success from sound business decisions based on a sound business mission. A "break-even" business doesn't make it to the winner's circle. In fact, with national inflation a constant business companion (historically 3% to 5% annually), any business that does not increase its net income to keep pace will see shrinking profit over time due to the inflationary creep of expenses, and declining income and profit spells doom for a business.

So, what will your business mission be?

1. Create ever-increasing sales, income, and profit.

    OR something else?

2. My mission is:

_____

_____

_____

_____

_____

_____

_____

_____

If you chose 1, fast forward to the next chapter and work on creating your business purpose. If you did not choose 1 and instead wrote a different mission statement, move to the next chapter but first bookmark this page for review. As you formulate your objectives in the coming exercises, you might decide to reconsider your business mission.

Before I conclude this chapter, I want to share an experience I had. Pressure from warm-hearted, well-intentioned associates once led me to soften my business mission and steer away from the hard objective of ever-increasing sales, income, and profit as my primary business mission. I softened my company's mission to: *continue generating new business activity that produces profit to share with our employees and also with the communities we live and work in.* Sounds good?

The result was: we lost focus, business faltered, and profits dipped. Fortunately, a quick return to a focus on increased income and profits for the business first and then others later, got my business back on the road to success—a road I never left again.

Focus your business decisions on fulfilling your business mission and purpose.

It is the same path you need to follow if you want to succeed as an entrepreneur.

Now, it's time for the next step: creating a business purpose.

Keep your smart phone, tablet, or laptop nearby so you can access an online dictionary as you write your business purpose and complete the exercises in this book. The words you use are critical because they trigger your thinking; thus you need to understand their meanings for them to lead you to positive business decisions.

CHAPTER 3

Creating a Business Purpose

"Think and grow rich!"

~ *Napoleon Hill*

EVEN THOUGH YOU HAVE A MISSION, YOU MUST ALSO formulate a purpose for your business. Why? Because a mission serves the needs of an entrepreneur while a business purpose serves the wants and needs of customers.

Purpose statements are sometimes referred to as "vision statements." *Vision* is defined as a vivid picture created by imagination (as in dreams).

Your business purpose is what you are aiming to do in order to fulfill the needs and wants of your customers.

Your business purpose defines how your company makes a difference in the world.

Purpose statements reflect the character and personality of you, the entrepreneur and business owner. The purpose becomes a published statement, a record of the company's intentions and commitments to suppliers, clients, vendors, customers, and prospective customers—in short, anyone you will target as a market for your products and services.

Successful entrepreneurs know their business purpose and are constantly working toward it.

A properly crafted business purpose is oftentimes incorporated into advertising and public relations. Some businesses proudly publish their purpose in bold lettering on company vehicles, on their website, on letterhead, in annual reports, and in sales materials.

In contrast, they usually remain silent about their business's mission and do not publicize it. Why? Because in some parts of society, wealth and profit have been demonized. Although large enterprises grab the lion's share of media attention, today even successful small businesses are starting to make headlines as profiteers. Ever-increasing sales, income, and profit are now considered somewhat taboo, even though they benefit society in many ways.

Without growing profits, businesses must eventually close their doors and jobs will disappear, but entrepreneurs worried about attracting ire and wrath often remain mute on their business mission.

Entrepreneurs aiming for success know it is profit and wealth that drive jobs, economic development, and ultimately a rise in living standards for all, but also know their customers are only interested in what will benefit them—so direct your business purpose at your customers.

What goes into a purpose statement?

Your purpose statement should express how you intend to do business and what benefits you want to provide your customers and clients. Step 1 is to write down the guiding principles that govern the business—these are your values (see form on page 42).

> *Principle* is defined as a moral belief or rule that helps you know what is right or wrong and that influences your actions; also a rule of conduct.

After you have written down your principles, review them. Can they be improved?

Step 2 is to commit your business ethics to paper (see the form on page 43). These are your rules of business behavior; and together with your principles, they are the **Standards of Excellence** that feed your business purpose.

Step 3 is to write down your commitments to customers and clients (see the form on page 44).

Step 1: Guiding Principles

(i.e., honesty, dependability, expertise)

_____

_____

_____

_____

_____

_____

_____

_____

_____

_____

_____

_____

Example of a Business Purpose Statement

"Stryker is one of the world's leading medical technology companies and is dedicated to helping healthcare professionals perform their jobs more efficiently while enhancing patient care. The company provides innovative orthopedic implants as well as state-of-the-art medical and surgical equipment to help people lead more active and satisfying lives."

Step 2: Business Ethics

(Your rules of business behavior)

_____

_____

_____

_____

_____

_____

_____

_____

_____

_____

_____

_____

Examples of Customer-Focused Principles

▲ The customer is always right.

▲ Always give more than your customers expect.

▲ Deliver exceptional service every time, every day, without fail.

▲ Never try to win an argument with a customer.

Step 3: Commitments to Customers and Clients

_____

_____

_____

_____

_____

_____

_____

_____

_____

_____

_____

_____

_____

_____

Example of a Business Purpose Statement:

Provide our customers with reasonably priced corporate health insurance that fits the current healthcare environment; and provide them with prompt, friendly, and knowledgeable service.

After you complete the first three steps, you will have the necessary information to formulate your Business Purpose Statement—**Step 4** (see the form on page 46).

Make your purpose statement action-oriented. Detail what you will deliver to customers. Write your purpose statement so your intended customer markets can clearly understand your meaning.

Realize that prospects, customers, clients, and vendors are watching you and evaluating your business performance.

Remember, your business purpose will most likely become a part of future advertising campaigns, whether you deal in print, web, or video media. So, review it and think hard about its impact on customers and prospects.

Pretend you're an existing customer or a new market you plan to target. Test what you drafted for accuracy and meaning.

Is the aim right? Do the words express what you mean? Does it promote your business in a positive way? Why or why not?

The next step is to be sure you know how to think and behave like a boss.

> **NOTE:** All of the forms in this book can be downloaded and printed in an 8.5-x-11-inch size by using this link:
> **www.growyourbusiness123.com/downloads.html**

Step 4: Business Purpose Statement

_____

_____

_____

_____

_____

_____

_____

_____

_____

_____

_____

_____

_____

_____

_____

_____

_____

_____

_____

_____

CHAPTER 4

Think and Behave (Manage) Like a Boss

"Change before you have to."

~ Jack Welch

A S AN ENTREPRENEUR YOU HAVE TWO JOBS. JOB NUMBER one is doing the work of the business—the skill you perform easily and should enjoy doing. For example, if you're an auto mechanic, it's fixing cars. If you're a custom cabinet maker, it's designing, constructing, selling, and installing cabinets. If you're a computer wizard, it's working with computer hardware and software. If you're an interior designer, maybe you specialize in home design or custom kitchens and bathrooms. You get the idea!

What is most overlooked, however, is an entrepreneur's other job: thinking like a boss and managing the business.

Being an entrepreneur entails deciding the right products and services you will make and sell, to whom you will market your goods and services, how you will advertise, how you will price your products and services to generate a profit you can live on (and pay employees a fair wage), how customer service will be conducted to retain customers, reviewing financial information, forecasting capital needs to support new product offerings, dealing with customer complaints and employee issues, responding to legal and government issues, etc.

Sounds like a lot—and it is! The first tool is **thinking and behaving like a boss**, which entails a different skill set than working the business—and it is critical to your business's growth and success. Neglecting the job of managing your business puts you at peril of losing the business.

The story that follows illustrates the struggle to move from a Phase 1 small business (where the focus is on doing the work of the business) to a Phase 2 small business (where the focus is on managing the business first; then doing the work of the business).

When my husband and I started our company, we quickly became wildly successful at helping small-business clients win government contracts. We were living the dream. It was just the two of us and we were doing what we loved doing—winning government contracts—the WORK of our business.

After a couple years, we started to notice that small things were being missed—things that didn't directly tie into winning contracts. Upon closer examination, we realized our business management efforts were sloppy, which led us to make a decision in 2010 to grow our business by hiring a support person to take on the administration and management tasks that were hollering for attention that we did not want to give.

Despite the wise counsel from a Small Business Development Center counselor, we underestimated how difficult the first hire would be. The added administrative responsibilities that come with having employees, i.e.; managing their activities, payroll functions, managing employee benefits, government reporting, Social Security, unemployment insurance, workman's compensation, etc., etc.

This was in the face of not effectively managing our business. We were obsessed with client service—which we are still proud of. But we did not allocate the time it took to lead, plan, budget, and dream what our business could become. We were so into DOING that we didn't take time to plan and MANAGE the business. This led to a haphazard growth strategy that impeded us.

By the end of 2011, with a staff of six, we were struggling. We lacked operating and managing procedures that would insure consistency and a company structure to support growth. Worse yet, we weren't listening to the story our numbers were telling us: our pricing model was flawed and getting in the way of profitability.

The result is, that, today our management plan and business structure is sound, and our numbers tell us stories that lead to successful results.

It's still hard. Small business ownership is not for the weak. But we are proud that we have moved into our growth phase, developed formal strategic plans, and can look confidently forward while maintaining our "scrappy" edge!

Susan Tellier, Owner, JetCo Solutions,
Grand Rapids, Michigan

The responsibility of managing the business is usually overlooked, treated as an interference to doing your job, and even sometimes ignored, by entrepreneurs— which results in the dismal small-business success rate of 20 percent.

How you manage these responsibilities and the decisions you make to remedy any issues or concerns is as important as doing the work of your business. Trust me. Having a Strategic Business Plan in place is the most important tool you can have when being the boss means you face daily business-management decisions.

A second important tool is **time management**. You will absolutely need to get a handle on how and where you spend your time for the business. Know this though: you already have all the time there is.

One behavior I incorporated while managing my businesses had to do with managers and employees who approached me with their ideas. Regardless if their idea was how to improve on a product, save manufacturing time, decrease expenses, or increase company profits, I often did not have time at that very moment to stop what I was doing and listen to them. Also, managers and staff liked to offer ideas but resisted doing the research and mental effort required to perfect an idea. They wanted me to do the heavy lifting of thinking out how their idea might improve our business functions. So, what I would do was thank the person for coming to me, but instead of listening to them at that time, I requested they put their thoughts in writing and explain how their idea would meet the goals of our Strategic Business Plan. Then, when they had done their homework and offered a written plan, I'd set aside time to read it and give their idea my complete attention and get back with them.

How often do you think they took the time and effort to do this? Not often! So, I didn't stifle ideas but I also managed my time more wisely. In other words, I was thinking and behaving like a boss.

You can't buy more time, or find extra time in the basement, or steal it from someone else.

People who say "I don't have enough time to spend on management activities" are simply not setting priorities nor managing their time effectively. Again, this is another reason why you should have a Strategic Business Plan, so that you know what issues are most important. (If you need additional assistance, there are plenty of books on time management. Visit www.growyourbusiness123.com for a list of suggested titles.)

A third tool is to **acknowledge when employees get it right**. Too many business owners are quick to point out when workers have erred or not delivered on a goal or promise, and then keep silent when employees get it right. It is the "no news is good news" mentality, which can have negative consequences on employee morale and ultimately their performance.

Remaining hush when an employee does a job well can significantly diminish and even defeat your efforts to get positive results.

Hopefully that is not how you operate your business because if you want to expand your business

YOU CANNOT DO IT ALL by yourself!

People expect a reward for successful efforts—when goals are achieved the individual and team must be compensated as promised. Tell employees how their contribution matters—remind them that the size of their paycheck is directly proportional to the progress they make.

You won't be sorry!

No entrepreneur wants to face the ever-present fear of insufficient income or funds to pay the bills and make payroll, or to purchase needed inventory and equipment, or to pay off their line of credit or business loan. But that is exactly what can happen if entrepreneurs don't have a Strategic Business Plan and if they don't manage like a boss.

To grow your business, you must be committed to thinking, planning, and behaving like the boss. Don't spend all (or most) of your time in job number one—WORKing the business The question is: who will fill the vacuum of management leadership when the entrepreneur spends the majority of his/her time working the business and soft peddles managing the business?

Be a winner. The survivors are the entrepreneurs who learn how to THINK business before doing business. They learn how to use strategic PLANNING to guide their decision-making to create ever-increasing sales, income, and profit—versus decisions, absent pre-thoughtfulness, that result in ever-shrinking sales, income, and profit!

In Stage Two, you will learn how to plan your business; beginning with the important business function called Research and Development.

STAGE II

How to PLAN Your Business

CHAPTER 5

Research & Development

**"If you don't have time to do it right,
you must have time to do it over."**

~ Anonymous

MOST LARGE BUSINESSES HAVE A RESEARCH AND DEVELOP-ment (R&D) department. Oftentimes companies have an entire division dedicated to the effort; complete with support staff, office space, and an operating budget. The job of the R&D team: identify potential markets and products/services that have a good chance of generating increased sales and income for the company and prepare strategic plans for presentation to senior management.

In contrast, most entrepreneurs and small business owners do not have dedicated R&D staff who are devoted to filling the pipeline with new markets, products, and services. No, most likely, you, the lone entrepreneur, are the R&D department.

What does R&D mean? What does an R&D department *really* do?

Typically R&D is a group of employees, apart from marketing and sales, charged with developing strategic plans, including identifying new products and markets. Usually it involves a willingness on the part of the business to forego current economic profit, in essence to wager or bet on future prosperity—but it is a calculated bet. Profitable businesses are constantly seeking knowledge about any existing and potential client base, customer needs and wants, and the economic climate. Then, with facts in hand, they evolve a plan—always with an eye on growth.

Research and Development is about learning what your prospective customers want and/or need—and then providing it to them.

As an example of how to gather market facts, let me share a bit of my business history …

Following an honorable discharge from the United States Air Force, I desperately needed to increase my monthly income. In a stroke of luck, an acquaintance who was a salesman suggested that I join his company. He sold home appliances on a commission basis and his commissions were quite lucrative.

I hired on, but after working there for only a short time, I uncovered an unfortunate truth: I did not know how to sell. As a result, I earned very low commissions. Because I had a family to support, I asked my more successful friend how and where he learned to sell. He subsequently invited me to a Dale Carnegie Sales Course (DCSC) demonstration meeting, where I enrolled in a full-course curriculum. (Finding the money for tuition was not easy!)

The classes did, indeed, teach me how to sell, but more

importantly, they imparted to me the value of reading. Each week the DCSC required class members to read books. I read Carnegie's *The Five Great Rules of Selling* and *How to Win Friends and Influence People,* along with *The Power of Positive Thinking* by Dr. Norman Vincent Peale. These books opened my mind to incredible possibilities for personal growth— and they inspired me.

Here's what I learned:

Anyone with drive and ambition can overcome ignorance and a lazy mind.

And, that the lame excuse:

I don't have time ...

... to read, study, research, explore, and learn new ways to improve is self-defeating.

My results surprised everyone—including me! My sales increased by over 400 percent, my commissions grew, and best of all, my wife and children were fed.

Armed with self-confidence and sales success, I was eager to tackle more. One Sunday morning, while reading the *Chicago Tribune,* I spotted an article touting the benefits of speed-reading. It claimed that within three weeks, an average reader could increase reading speed and comprehension 200 to 400 percent by following a simple do-it-yourself plan.

Well, I practiced the lessons in the *Chicago Tribune* and my reading speed improved daily. Today, I now read seventy to ninety books annually—these include fiction, which I devour for entertainment, and numerous informative texts focused on running a business, planning, etc. The business books I read cover the functions of marketing, R&D, merchandising, finance, administration, customer service, taxes, recordkeeping, etc. Each book adds to my knowledge of different business functions that follow strategic business planning.

What you "know" is the cornerstone of R&D.

Reading opens your mind to new opportunities and countless possibilities. After reading certain books, you will wonder "What if we … ?" or "How can we … ?" So, make time to read. The information you gain will vastly improve your R&D performance and odds of success.

Set aside at least one hour every day to read something new about your industry, markets, product trends, fad products that are disappearing, emerging fad products, new discoveries, etc.

Even 15-minute intervals for reading will expand your R&D results. Open your mind and feed it with new information!

As an entrepreneur and business owner, **you have two choices:** grow your business or watch it slowly fade and die. There is no standing still in the business world—change is ever-present! And R&D is the tool to use in managing change.

Sure, some businesses manage to float for a year or two, but with inflation a constant reality that increases your expenses, no one can do it for long. Any business unable to expand profitably will eventually fold.

Change is unavoidable.

Most successful entrepreneurs thrive on the challenge change provides, but we also sometimes enjoy the comfort predictability provides when we run a business. Let's be honest: knowing what to expect feels good and safe—and it's easy. Perhaps showered with some early successes, you now believe things will remain the same, unwavering—you expect current success to remain and see no need to change course or action, but that is a misguided expectation.

Change is necessary for survival.

When you read about a small business that has succeeded in the long run, business transformation—*change*—is always a part of the story.

The clock is ticking. Change happens every second, whether you actively participate in it or not. Look around. Read the news. Every day thousands of small businesses take root in the United States, with smart, energetic vision-aries—people like you—at the helm. Likewise, somewhere else a firm files for bankruptcy, merges with another company, sells out to a competitor, or simply closes its doors. That's what I call "the business river of life," or if you prefer, "business churn."

You and I are somewhere in the middle of the river. We are the enterprising thinkers, the folks who run today's small businesses and at any given moment some of us are struggling to stay afloat while others are on the brink of a new product or service or a major market expansion or acquisition of a competitor. It is true that change is unavoidable, but as an active participant in your business, you will have the benefit of choice and there are two sides to pick from: become a victim—that's what I call "bad change" or become a change agent—"good change."

Change agents have an eye on the future, are motivated and inspiring, and see the unleashed potential in their current surroundings. Victims follow and often get swallowed by their prey.

So, what is it going to be? Do you want to become a change agent or not?

On the following pages, I provide a four-step blueprint for R&D—what I call the **Business Espionage Intelligence Plan** (BEIP)—or *beep* as my staff pronounced it!

Espionage is a noun and refers to spying, which typically involves watching for an event and trying to gather information. By setting up a formal BEIP you will, in essence, be spying on your competitors, customers, and prospects to gather information about their products and services and their wants and needs. Note—this data is all legally obtained and gives you knowledge you can use to your benefit.

Gathering accurate data is the most important part of the R&D process.

I suggest you use either a three-ring binder or develop a spreadsheet in Excel to organize your BEIP data.

STEP 1

Collect, record, and then analyze the customers, products, services, and marketing programs of your competitors.

If you don't have any competitors, constantly evaluate what is going on in your primary market(s) that can impact the sales of your products and services. This is an integral part of any research and development effort and should occur on a regular basis.

You must know your customers and your competitors.

STEP 2

After mining for the above data, examine your findings and analyze the data by asking questions. Here are some questions to get you started.

▲ What can I do with the information I acquired to profitably impact our sales?

▲ What markets or trends are my competitors tapping into that I have not considered?

▲ Is there a new service or product I can offer to a similar customer base?

▲ Where are my competitors' customers coming from? Online? Brick-and-mortar stores? Referrals?

▲ Are there demographic market shifts my competitors are exploiting?

▲ What can I learn by segmenting geographic and age-related sales data? Do older buyers only purchase product A while younger purchasers buy A with B and sometimes C? What do these trends tell me?

▲ How can my business benefit before market saturation occurs (i.e., the end of a product fad)?

▲ What do my customers and prospects want or need? How are other companies filling the need?

STEP 3

"Think" ahead of your competitors by regularly repeating steps 1 and 2.

The steady supply of new and existing market information you obtain will begin to fuel *real* development for your business. It is not enough to simply collect the information. You must record it and look at the data and dig for the morsels. You just might hit gold—and when you do, you can score big!

STEP 4

Create a Spy Book, to store the information you gather. This book is an important strategic business planning tool. The Spy Book is either a part of your BEIP three-ring binder, indexed with five tabs as follows, or you can develop a spreadsheet in Excel:

1. New Product Ideas
2. Existing Product Ideas
3. New Services We Can Sell
4. New Markets to Explore
5. Existing Markets to Improve

A series of forms inserted behind each tab documents the important information you learn from business associates and others met throughout the course of social events and doing business. An example entry is below. (A sample form is provided on page 64.)

Date	Source	Information Collected	Action
7/30/2015	Joe K.–friend of Sam.	has product that does X, Y, Z	Buy one and explore how we can use it to improve our sales.

You must be an advocate for your business. You are the entrepreneur—the leader—and it is *your job* to be interested in your industry and what your competitors are doing.

Realize, this research is a part of that other job you have— **THINKING** like a boss. It is not your WORK job.

Whenever the opportunity arises, ask colleagues at seminars, local Chamber of Commerce functions, Small Business Association events, and other networking occasions open-ended questions so that you can learn. A question requiring only a yes or no answer won't yield anything new. Ask: What products do you sell? How long have you been in business? Is your firm having trouble retaining an elderly customer base? Etc.

Always remember to update your Spy Book so the information can be reviewed during your quarterly and annual Strategic Plan Reviews (see chapter 10).

NOTE: All of the forms in this book can be downloaded and printed in an 8.5-x-11-inch size by using this link: **www.growyourbusiness123.com/downloads.html**

SPY BOOK INFORMATION

Date	Source	Information Collected	Action

Date	Source	Information Collected	Action

Date	Source	Information Collected	Action

Date	Source	Information Collected	Action

Here are two tools I used to insure I was making the right business decisions:

Tool No. 1

The most important management responsibility for entrepreneurs is Strategic Business Planning. R&D is the critical tool in learning/knowing exactly how to make strategic decisions that will increase sales, income, and profit.

Tool No. 2

Test every decision (*every single one*). HOW? State the decision you are considering and ask yourself:

▲ **Will the decision I'm considering increase sales?**

▲ **Will it increase income?**

▲ **Will it increase profits?** (These are the three critical elements of your mission statement!)

If you can honestly answer yes to this three-part question, proceed to a second question: Will the decision I'm considering result in satisfying and/or fulfilling the needs and wants of my prospects/customers? (Your business purpose!)

If you can answer yes to both questions, you are on the right track and probably have a winning decision, and you can proceed with confidence knowing it is based on sound data rather than guesswork and intuition alone.

Simply capturing research data is not enough; you must analyze it and use it to direct your business decisions—the *development* phase of R&D.

Development assumes the existence of a product or service prototype. You have the idea for the service and if it's a product, you have a concept or prototype in hand. During this phase, you will identify the steps necessary to bring the new offering to market.

But what if there is no tangible product or service prototype? Then you must first research the idea to see if the concept is viable before establishing steps leading to development.

All R&D efforts require the commitment of time, labor, and money. Yes, you must "wager" resources, but remember it is a calculated bet, unlike spinning a roulette wheel in Las Vegas. When we talk about the entrepreneurial garden, R&D is one of the seeds a successful business plants; seeds of future sales, income, and profit. A failure to plant seeds now might mean you end up having nothing to harvest later.

Commitment to R&D offers a payoff. The bounty you will receive is the discovery of which new products, services, and markets offer the best outcomes—the highest probability of success with "success" measured by potential for increased company sales, income, and profit.

**Root your decisions in fact.
Engage in ample research to ensure
you are not simply rolling the dice.**

Performing R&D is a necessary way to spend time and resources. When done correctly, R&D will significantly reduce the potential risk of failure when you introduce new products and services and/or expand into other markets.

Allocating resources (time, effort, and money) to R&D must be a management priority for entrepreneurs.

What follows is a proven method I used as part of my R&D process, prior to defining company Objectives. It is a mental, mind-dumping exercise to help assess your current business environment. As a leader, you should know what is going on with your business. Now, take what you know and organize it in your BEIP binder, as this will become the template for creating business objectives down the road.

Sound easy? When you do the homework, it is!

Problems and Opportunities—the third Tool of R&D

Start by formulating a list of your business's **P's & O's**— PROBLEMS and OPPORTUNITIES. Use your employees to help build the list. I sent a copy of the form to each employee and asked them to offer what they saw as P's and O's for our business, and required they respond within a week. (Most felt complimented that I asked for their input.)

As you work through this exercise, you will find that problems often point to or suggest new opportunities and ideas; some that you might not have considered before.

As you move through the exercise, watch for these important links. Eventually these "idea seedlings" will couple with other new opportunities and feed the development of business objectives. For now, though, just do the exercise. Below are a few examples of P's & O's from some of my R&D efforts.

PROBLEMS	OPPORTUNITIES
Sales of new products are slow	Advertise to new markets; add new sales personnel
Income was soft last year	Re-price products and services
Expenses are growing and sales are stagnant	Reduce labor costs via computer
Prospecting results are diminishing	Allocate more time and resources to look for new products and/or services
Lack enough qualified employees to service customers	Set higher hiring and training targets
Having to repay borrowed capital from profits	Limit your company to borrowing only one month's operating capital, and repay it before borrowing again. Guards against escalating debt and your avoidance of expense control

Now it's your turn. Using the blank form on page 69 or ones downloaded from www.growyourbusiness123.com, list your P's & O's. Then share what you've compiled, first with a spouse if an active participant in the business; followed by managers, key employees, and business advisers; including accountants, bankers, and perhaps a trusted attorney. Work on the list until you are sure it is on target. (With the expediency of e-mail, you can do this quickly.)

Don't be concerned if this exercise exposes different and sometimes conflicting perspectives about your business

NOTE: All of the forms in this book can be downloaded and printed in an 8.5-x-11-inch size by using this link:
www.growyourbusiness123.com/downloads.html

PROBLEMS & OPPORTUNITIES

PROBLEMS	OPPORTUNITIES

conditions, because you will learn to discern the difference between real versus imagined P's & O's—these views would not necessarily come to light without doing this exercise.

After reviewing the product and market information in your Spy Book, and armed with a P's & O's list that satisfies you, you are now ready to identify and create company objectives for the upcoming year—the first step toward strategizing an action plan for your business.

Let's get started.

CHAPTER 6

Developing Objectives

"**Don't agonize. Organize.**"

~ Florynce Kennedy

B EFORE YOU CAN TAKE ADVANTAGE OF THE OPPORTUNITIES that will give you the greatest chance to increase sales, income, and profit …

You need to identify the business targets that must be met in order to resolve any problems.

That's right. Developing Business Objectives utilizes the P's & O's you identified in the previous chapter.

You can formulate your Business Objectives in four easy steps.

STEP 1

Review the objectives I wrote for one of my companies, as this will give you an idea of what objectives should be like.

▲ Develop and initiate a plan (in concert with our bank) to meet capital needs and finance growth over the next one to three years.

▲ Continue to upgrade financial-information software to assist in keeping our company financially sound.

▲ Accelerate our income and profit growth via increased sales in expanded markets, targeting 10% growth each year.

▲ Create and stage an ongoing employee-training program.

▲ Deliver prompt, friendly, and knowledgeable customer services via employee training and education.

▲ Improve our advertising and public relations programs to maintain and increase our customer base.

▲ Have fun and enjoy our work.

Next, review each business *function* and consider what the most important business issue is that needs your attention in order to produce the best results.

**Function is defined as
the special purpose or action
for which a thing exists.**

Following are the seven functions of business, and their principle actions, in chronological order, as they occur in the business process.

FUNCTION	PRINCIPLE ACTIVITIES
1st: MARKETING	Determine your products and services, the markets you will sell them in, and the advertising that communicates with your markets.
2nd: SALES	Create prospect sales presentations that will satisfy the wants and needs of your target markets.
3rd: BUSINESS ADMINISTRATION	Process customer/client sales, product delivery, customer services; and maintenance of the company's master data system.
4th: HUMAN RESOURCES	Hire and train employees; and management of government programs (Social Security, etc.).
5th: INFORMATION TECHNOLOGY	Research and implement new hardware, software, and IT training that will increase company productivity and profits.
6TH: MANUFACTURING/SERVICES PRODUCTION	Produce quality products and services in a timely manner, and resolve product failures.
7th: FINANCE/ACCOUNTING/TAXES	Produce timely operations and financial records, government-required reporting, and tax obligations.

©2016 GYB123

Organize your Business Objectives, according to the seven functions of business, by utilizing the form provided on page 74.

OBJECTIVES

Date:

1. Marketing Function:

2. Sales Function:

3. Business Administration Function:

4. Human Resources Function:

5. Information Technology Function:

6. Manufacturing/Production Function:

7. Finance/Accounting/Taxes: Function

©2016 GYB123

List at least one objective for each function and describe what you will do for each to gain positive results for your business.

Additionally, I developed a **"standards of performance"** (see the chart on page 76) to use when measuring the results in each function of business—you should consider doing this as well. It is a great management tool.

A business's financial plan develops from the enterprise's Strategic Business Plan. The same holds true for a company's employee-training, marketing, sales, and customer service plans.

All action plans are subordinate offshoots of the master Strategic Business Plan.

STEP 2

Refer to the P's & O's you developed in the previous chapter and write down the business objectives you just identified. Regardless if you have been carrying these objectives around for months as scribbles on the back of a business card or tucked inside your head, it does not matter.

NOTE: All of the charts and forms in this book can be downloaded and printed in an 8.5-x-11-inch size by using this link:
www.growyourbusiness123.com/downloads.html

STANDARDS OF PERFORMANCE	
FUNCTIONS	**STANDARDS OF PERFORMANCE**
1st: MARKETING	Determine what your clients and prospects need and/or want; then give it to them.
2nd: SALES	Create product and service descriptions that are the truth, the whole truth, and nothing but the truth. Also, couple each product fact with its related buyer benefit.
3rd: BUSINESS ADMINISTRATION	Achieve 100 percent accuracy in our master data system information and execute customer services that are prompt, friendly, and knowledgeable.
4th: HUMAN RESOURCES	Identify and acquire the brightest, smartest, and ambitious team-playing employees via hiring and training programs that identify candidates.
5th: INFORMATION TECHNOLOGY	Focus on acquiring information on the latest and best hardware, software, and IT-employee training information that will reduce expenses and increase our productivity and profits.
6th: MANUFACTURING/ SERVICES PRODUCTION	Achieve near 100 percent quality products and services in a timely manner and promptly resolve any that do not perform well.
7th: FINANCE/ ACCOUNTING/TAXES	Produce operation reports within 5 working days of close of monthly business; produce financial records within 10 days of monthly, quarterly close of business; attended with analysis of the areas showing up or down results; and prepare federal and state tax returns that record every penny of income and take every dollar of expense.

©2016 GYB123

I used these Standards of Performance to manage my key employees, including managers. **You should publish and use these Standards as your principle management tool when measuring employee performance!**

Now, it is time to make your objectives real by writing them on the Objectives form.

STEP 3

If you have been actively participating in the *Growing Your Business 1, 2, 3* process, you are now ready to compare problems and opportunities with the objectives you stated on the Objectives form. Do they connect?

Do you see opportunities that relate to the challenges of the objectives listed?

Example:

Objective #3 in the master Strategic Business Plan for one of my business operations stated: "Develop a marketing plan that gets results."

The original objective I pursued didn't yield the results I wanted. So, I talked with an expert, someone I trusted within my firm, a manager named Don Werme, who introduced me to Carlton Reade, the inventor of the waxed milk carton. After explaining some details, I asked Carlton what he would do to improve marketing and get better results. After all, the wax milk carton was a hit and any advice he offered had solid experience to back it up. His answer was simple:

**"Discover what your prospects want
and/or need, then give it to them!"**

~Carlton Reade

If you do, they will buy from you, GUARANTEED!

I took his advice, revised my marketing objectives—and boy o' boy, did it produce positive results.

Determining what your customers want is the trick. It takes time to research what existing and prospective customers desire.

Seek input from the people around you—managers, employees, customers, and others whose opinions you value and trust. Their input should provide you with fresh ideas for your business objectives and help you determine what your customers really want or need—instead of you *guessing* what they want or need.

R&D efforts are the key to discovering what your customers want or need.

STEP 4

Time for the acid test! Read each objective out loud and then ask yourself:

▲ Why do this objective?

▲ Will this objective support our business mission? Does it or will it increase sales, income, and profit?

▲ Does this objective fit in with our business purpose?

If you answered yes, move to the next objective. If you answered no, then rework the objective until you can answer yes.

The first time you write down your objectives, you will need to focus, concentrate, and pay attention to detail. Press on. Don't give up. With each yearly repetition, the process will flow more easily; and objectives, once on target, should not require much alteration from year to year. Some objectives will even remain unchanged.

Now, take a look back. You have created your business MISSION, your business PURPOSE, and a list of business OBJECTIVES.

You have built the foundation for creating a master Strategic Action Plan—what I consider to be the creative and fun part!

CHAPTER 7

Formulating a
Strategic Action Plan

**"A business 'garden' won't grow without
the 'fertilizer' of strategic planning."**

~ Richard B. Sanford

THIS STEP OF THE STRATEGIC BUSINESS PLAN REQUIRES YOU to use your imagination. *Imagination* is "the act or power of forming a mental image of something not present to the senses or not previously known or experienced—in short, a mental image or creation of the mind."

Strategizing is the fun part
of business planning.

This is when you get to dream a future for your business—although afterward you will need to "wake up" so you can focus on market facts and create specific strategies to drive your business toward your mission of ever-increasing sales, income, and profit.

Because action plans emerge from strategies, let's first define what strategies are. A *strategy* is like a road map, but instead of being a graphic illustration using arrows and other symbols, it is words in paragraph form.

A strategy describes in specific terms what you need to do to accomplish the objective that you WANT to achieve.

Action plans involve more detail. Action plans describe HOW the work will be done, WHO will do it, and WHEN an activity will happen—and always with an eye on the desired objective.

STRATEGIC ACTION PLANS are composed of four parts and answer these questions:

1. What do you **WANT** to do? What result do you want to achieve? A definitive strategy, carefully worded, will outline an action plan that answers this question. *(Example: We want to increase sales this year by 10 percent. We will do so by adding three salespeople and expanding our sales bonus plan.)*

2. **HOW** will you do it? Describe the steps you will take to accomplish the strategy you outlined in number 1. *(Example: We will advertise for the open sales positions and interview candidates, hiring the three who are best qualified to succeed. Also ask your staff to develop an expanded sales bonus plan.)*

3. **WHO** is responsible for the work undertaken in each step? You must assign people to specific tasks. *(Example: Joe Smith in human resources, Ann Jones in business administration, and Sam Butler in sales.)*

4. **WHEN** will the work be done? Identify specific completion dates for the steps you outlined in number 2. *(Example: place advertisement within thirty days; hire three salespeople within sixty days; and have expanded sales bonus plan ideas submitted within forty-five days.)*

This process is what I call the "WANT, HOW, WHO, and WHEN" of strategic planning. In essence, you determine the actions needed to accomplish your company's mission, purpose, and objectives. Then, you outline a series of steps necessary to accomplish each strategy and to whom tasks are assigned; and finally, you create a timeline with interval benchmarks to reach project completion by the targeted date.

No longer must you rely on unproven ideas, guesses, intuition, or well-meaning but uniformed input from associates, employees, family members, and friends who are convinced they know how to solve your business-growth challenges.

I realize that most entrepreneurs in the process of moving from a Phase 1 small business to a Phase 2 small business, where expansion requires additional employees to support growth, probably build their first master Strategic Business

Plan alone since they don't have managers or other key employees to assist in the process. My initial attempt at strategic planning was like this—I did it by myself—which was okay.

In a Phase 1 small business, the entrepreneur drives the business forward and is responsible for making *all* decisions and directing *all* of his and employees' work.

Entrepreneurs typically enjoy calling the shots and thus making plans alone seems like a natural extension of running a start-up business—but working in a vacuum when you reach Phase 2 status can have unintended negative results.

When a small business grows into Phase 2, owners are confronted with new hurdles—specific management challenges surrounding growth and innovation, challenges that might not have been visible while still a Phase 1 small business where they focused on doing the **WORK** of the business.

As your small business blooms, the focus will change from a mindset of "I make this happen" to a new one of "I must get positive business results through the actions and efforts of myself and others.

In Phase 2, the workforce typically has expanded along with management. Work is more complicated. The owner must impart business philosophy, his or her way of doing things, and strategic business plans for growth to managers who will convey these messages to the people they manage. At critical times, the owner will also speak directly to managers and employees as it is imperative that the owner *clearly communicate* the company's wants and needs (your Strategic Business Plan details) to staff to ensure that desired performance, quality, and other business goals are met.

At this juncture, Strategic Action Plans take a central role in managing a Phase 2 small business.

Put down your pencil. Read what follows and let it soak in.

You must commit to making STRATEGIES and ACTION PLANS the tools of your management process; not just a priority— but the #1 priority—for running your business. This is the only dependable path to expansion and success.

Strategic Action Plans *will* lead your business to success if you follow the steps in this book. When properly done, strategic planning will direct you toward more profitable products and services and away from less profitable ones. It will push you to explore expanding markets and turn away from market trends (fads) that are in decline. It will help you discover advertising niches to reach the markets you want to capture and highlight opportunities to reject because they sport no advantage.

Strategic planning also identifies the support activities that must be in place to achieve success: who needs training in what, which areas of your business need more administrative support staff, new hardware and software needs, etc.

Failure is not the first choice for any business—but in an expanding business, failure can fast become a reality if you do not follow a strategic business plan when making business decisions.

Planning is never easy. It involves what the great Austrian-American economist Joseph Schumpeter called "creative destruction,"[1] a constant churn in how you do business, always with an eye on innovation, new techniques, new technology, and sometimes—new employees, and any experts you may need to bring onboard to get the results you want. You may even need to drop products, services, markets, and staff if they aren't generating the desired results. This requires some 'courage and forward thinking'.

Did I use this technique in my businesses? Absolutely. It worked best when I set aside early morning hours, before my "real" workday started. I am a morning person by nature and that time of day worked best for me.

"It wasn't raining when Noah built the Ark! Anticipating change helps you to manage the thinking you will need to do to stay ahead of changes that can either assist your company's growth or defeat your efforts at survival."

~ David Rhoa, President of West Michigan Mailers

---

1. Schumpeter, J. A. *Capitalism, Socialism and Democracy*, 3rd ed (New York: Harper & Row) 1950 p. 81.

Do you work best in the morning, afternoon, or evening? Find your most productive creative time and invite key staff to meet with you.

Schedule multiple sessions in advance and request that everyone who was invited attends—with NO excuses except for certain family commitments or illnesses.

Because I sent out a pre-meeting memo, with a complete agenda; and periodic date reminders, my staff knew I was serious and committed to strategic planning. If you do the same, yours will too.

By now you are probably asking, "Okay, how do I get started? How do I actually formulate a Strategic Action Plan for my business?"

Here's how I did it ...

In the beginning, I tried using traditional information resources: the Internet, library, college experts, and university think tanks. Ample experts with letters after their names offered advice I couldn't use. Other experts focused on the functions of business, touting software to buy, computer mainframes to lease, and back-up servers with 100% assurance to prevent data loss; while others offered advice on how to do R&D on a global scale.

Here's the problem: I wasn't looking to buy equipment. I wasn't global. And I wasn't a big business. I was a little guy, just getting started on building a Phase 2 small business, and like many entrepreneurs, I didn't have the resources—human or financial—to do that kind of strategic planning.

As I reviewed thick texts written by peer-nominated experts, I saw how complicated strategic planning and building action plans could be when presented in a Big-Biz format. Small business is all about doing "big" while working "simple"; so the tools and texts the experts directed me to when I was conducting my research had to be narrowed in scope if an entrepreneur like me was going to use them successfully.

I found one book written by Dale McConkey and an adult education management course by Dale Carnegie that somewhat described the process of strategic planning. Bookstore shelves weren't swelling with the sort of how-to guides in *simplified* Strategic Business Planning I needed back then—and certainly none that were written by entrepreneurs with a proven track record in the small business world.

Carnegie's text did a good job of defining elements of formal strategic planning and McConkey's book, *How to Manage By Results*, offered some of what I needed, but by the fifth chapter it shifted toward a big business approach. Thus I saw a need to develop something for my small businesses—something other small businesses could also use, something *simplified*—and that's how my Strategic Business Plan Model and the Strategic Action Plan outline I share with you below became a reality.

Do the tools work?

Yes! I can prove it. I have proved it. I used these tools to grow eleven small businesses—each a business I founded. Most became Phase 2 businesses; several I sold; a couple I closed their doors; and two grew much larger, with one, the Sanford Insurance Group Inc., a third-party insurance administration company, generating over $136 million in annual sales revenue.

The following exercise describes how you can design a Strategic Action Plan for your business in five simple steps.

Developing a Strategic Action Plan

STEP 1

Assemble your team in a secluded location so everyone can work without any distractions. (In the beginning, my team consisted of my spouse, two employees, and myself.) Enforce **NO** interruptions and all cell phones **OFF**!

> **"You have to learn to treat people as a resource. ... Don't ask 'what do they cost?' but rather 'what is the yield? What can they produce for you?'"**
> ~ *Peter F. Drucker*

You will need to allocate two to three hours for the first planning session, as there should be an adequate amount of time for strategizing. Subsequent strategic planning sessions will require much less time because the planning team will have become acquainted with the process. However, don't shortchange yourself on time or you might end up shortchanging your business's future.

At one of the first companies I started, I found myself struggling to find time for strategic planning. (Time is a constraint placed on all humans, but we entrepreneurs seem particularly lacking in it.) One day, Bill Hamilton, a business associate and friend, took me aside and told me a story that set me straight and taught me the value of prioritizing to make the best use of my time. The moral of his story: *People set priorities for what they deem important in life and will make time for it.*

MAKE TIME FOR PLANNING YOUR BUSINESS FUTURE!

STEP 2

Read out loud to those gathered your business mission, business purpose, and business objectives as recorded. (If you have been doing your homework, this information should be completed and accessible on the forms provided in this book or from my website.)

Reviewing this information first will focus your planning team on the specific subject of Strategic Business Planning—and away from where their minds are when they entered the meeting room; i.e., kids, arguments from the breakfast table, work left on their desk yesterday, a hot prospect they expect to see and close today, etc., etc.

STEP 3

Evaluate each objective one at a time by asking *"What can we do to accomplish this objective?* The answers will become your strategies. Solicit and encourage input from the entire group—new ideas and lots of them!

Use an easel or whiteboard and list each of your company's objectives followed by the ideas and strategies that are offered. (This is called *storyboarding* and was invented by Walt Disney.)

Write the strategies beneath each objective listed—include all ideas, even wild and seemingly impossible ones.

To prevent squashing the creative process, allow no criticism of anyone's input.

STEP 4

Instruct the participants to review the strategies on the board (provided in step 3) and rank them from 1 to 10, in order of importance. Have them write down their rankings. When everyone has finished doing this, then have all of the participants share their responses with the group. As the rankings are shared write the number beside each strategy listed on the white board.

A picture will emerge. Those strategies that have the most team support will become evident.

Later, in the privacy of your office, it is your turn to review the strategies. Which ideas do *you* believe will move your business toward ever-increasing sales, income, and profit? Which ideas will best solve a problem or obstacle your business is facing? Which ideas will allow you to exploit a new opportunity to your advantage?

You then decide what priority to assign each listed strategy. Move the items identified as a high priority to the top of the list and act on them immediately.

Keep a record of all these strategies for future reference. When I reviewed my action plans a year later, some of the noted ideas became viable and profitable business opportunities. Plus the record served as validation of the effort expended in creating a plan.

In short, strategic business planning works.

STEP 5

After your winnowing process, re-assemble your planning team and focus on the strategies you selected as having the most promise. Begin the meeting with "let's consider the strategies I selected from our meeting and moved to the top of the list." Remember, these are the WHAT. You must visualize the steps that will accomplish the strategy. Make it real by writing down the steps. HOW will you do the jobs that need doing? WHO will you assign to each task? Write down the names of each person responsible, for all to see. Next, determine WHEN the project will be completed. What is the targeted timeline?

Be specific. No fudging on when the Action is to be finished!

After this follow-up meeting, congratulate yourself. You have just created an action plan, and a terrific management tool for making good stuff happen!

On the facing page is a sample action planning form that is useful for recording information described in the five action-planning steps. Fill in the form with one or more strategies for each identified objective.

Note: If you have already progressed from a Phase 1 small business to a Phase 2 small business, perhaps you have added employees, managers, and line staff to serve your business expansion. At this point, an often subtle but vital mental debate ensues: do you include a spouse who is active in the business, key employees, managers, and outside advisers (accountant and banker, for example) in the

---

NOTE: All of the forms in this book can be downloaded and printed in an 8.5-x-11-inch size by using this link:
www.growyourbusiness123.com/downloads.html

Strategic Action Plan

Company: _____ Date: _____

Action Plan for Business Year: _____

Objective 1 (Want)	Strategy 1 (How/steps to take)	Assignment (Who)	Target Dates (When)
	Strategy 2	Assignment	Target Dates
Objective 2	Strategy 1	Assignment	Target Dates
	Strategy 2	Assignment	Target Dates

93

strategic-planning process? You must decide this on your own as all businesses are different. In my case, my wife was able to provide valuable common sense to our strategic-planning activities; so I included her in our planning sessions.

The first company I formed was RBSA Inc., a financial services company. I needed outside advice to reach the potential I envisioned for its future. I didn't know where to start—but start I did; and gradually, through experience, I developed this model for Strategic Action Plans that can be incorporated into any business. I used it to accelerate growth in the many firms I started during my career. It worked for me, and it will work for you.

Strategic Business Planning Takes Time

Strategic business planning is part of your management job and it is time consuming. You also need input from managers and key employees, plus their commitment to assist with the plan, which will temporarily pull them away from other important business functions. However, there will be a payday. A successful business needs cohesiveness—everyone working with the same blueprint, the same plan, and the same goals.

Without a clearly written Strategic Action Plan, managers and employees are engaged in what I call "motion without meaning"; sometimes referred to as "running around in circles." And that is a prescription for disaster.

You might need to remind your team that you, the owner, have the deciding vote when it comes to key decisions on which strategies to pursue, which to postpone, and which to abort. You must have the final say on which strategies will best accomplish your business objectives—after all, it is your company.

But do not make decisions in a vacuum. A solid Strategic Action Plan involving key employees and advisers will ensure that you don't.

Warning: It is easy to be distracted by stories of quick profits or dreams of easy-selling products and turn away from your Strategic Business Plan, especially when positive results are slow in coming. Don't do it!

These distractions are paths to failure. The quick-and-easy, fast-buck stories are 95% pie-in-the-sky fantasies that suck up time, energy, and money with little reward.

I have found that entrepreneurs eager for results and often pressed for time are easily led away from the action plans they worked so hard to develop. Get-rich-quick schemes seem to present themselves in the course of doing business, and can potentially divert you away from your company's goals. This, ultimately, will diminish your efforts and focus, and send mixed messages to managers and employees about what your company's Strategic Action Plan really is.

There are no shortcuts to success.

So, **"plan your work and work your plan"**—sage advice, as true today as it was when Vince Lombardi said it years ago. If you want to see results, you must stay the course, even when traversing through rough waters. Adjust your Strategic Business Plan as needed but *only* after careful and thoughtful consideration.

Now, it is time to WORK your business, utilizing the Strategic Action Plans you developed so you can enjoy ever-increasing sales, income, and profit.

STAGE III

How to WORK Your Business

CHAPTER 8

Introducing Your Strategic Action Plan

"Don't worry about people stealing your ideas. If your ideas
are any good, you'll have to ram them down
people's throats to get them to accept them!"

~Howard Aiken

I T IS TIME TO COMMUNICATE YOUR STRATEGIC ACTION PLAN TO the key advisers, managers, and employees who will assist you in carrying out your expansion goals. These individuals are the people you will depend on to help you achieve ever-increasing sales, income, and profit for the business.

Sharing this information can be a tough step for some entrepreneurs. Most business owners regularly think about their business plans but do not openly share the information with the employees who can help move the company forward for fear of someone stealing their ideas.

When you develop a Strategic Business Plan, you stand at a great divide, a crossing, where you must transition from being a one-man or one-woman style of management to a leader-manager approach. No longer is your business a solo operation. To complete this transition, you will need to relinquish some control and decision-making, along with some day-to-day administrative duties, to others—but with your oversight. And this includes sharing your Strategic Action Plan.

After a certain point, delegating responsibility is the only way you can profitably expand a business. There are only twenty-four hours in a day and your time and energy are limited. So, you will need to enlist others in your organization to share the load—people you trust—to help make growth happen.

To grow your business, you will have to eventually enlist help from others in your organization—people you trust—by sharing your business strategies and action plans.

You might think: *Hey, wait a minute! Turn over some control? Share my business secrets and strategic plans with key employees? What if they leave and take what I've worked so hard to develop with them?*

Most business owners are cautious when confronted with the need to share their strategies with managers and employees. It is true, employees could leave and yes, perhaps there is opportunity for them to take your ideas out the door when they go. What if they start their own business or go to work for the competition? What happens then? Fear not! Competition keeps an entrepreneur sharp, always looking forward, and on target with their Strategic Action Plan.

Whenever you share confidential information, there is

risk. Usually you will share information with your managers—the people you have promoted based on their decision-making ability, level-headedness in the face of pressure, and entrepreneurial spirit.

Keep in mind, though, sharing information also offers the opportunity for enormous reward in the form of improved employee performance, increased sales, and greater profit.

These people are managers because they are leaders, and leaders can and sometimes do leave for greener pastures or to start their own businesses. However, I think the risk is minimal and worth the gains received—it certainly proved advantageous in my businesses. I never viewed the possibility of an employee moving to a competitor or branching out on his or her own as a problem. In fact, I always saw it as an opportunity. Hear me out.

I viewed managers and employees who took the initiative to carry out my Strategic Business Plan as opportunists. I liked them. They were go-getters who made good things happen and were interested in the success of my company *and* their personal success. They had vision and a knack for doing what was required to make the business successful— and when they delivered, I rewarded them accordingly.

Furthermore, because I used a fair and equitable compensation system rooted in performance, most of my top employees stayed with me; and thus, my companies continued to grow. But, of course, the decision is yours.

Look into your crystal ball. Where do you want your business to be in three to five years? Down for the count or standing strong in front of the competition? If you want the latter, take my lead and share what you know with your trusted advisers and employees—it is a necessary step for growing a business.

Additionally, I urged my employees and managers to identify their replacements and mentor them forward.

I told them, "You can't move up in a growing company if you don't have a qualified replacement for your job." This strategy allowed for a fluid transition when a management function changed leadership and it encouraged everyone to work at their highest potential.

Yes, I admit some of my key employees, the very people I mentored along in their careers, did leave to start small businesses. To each I always gave my blessing and support. Why? Because this attitude of goodwill paid off. My company was popularly referred to as "a great place to work; where one can get ahead in life." The reputation and respect I earned inspired numerous high-quality, energetic individuals to pursue jobs at my companies—and many of our best job applicants were referred by current and former employees.

So, share your Strategic Action Plan with managers and employees. Be sure to stress what their specific roles and responsibilities are and explain why they are required to participate in monthly, quarterly, and annual reviews of their goals and performance; as well as the company's goals and what results were achieved or missed.

The next step: implementation of strategies and actions.

CHAPTER 9

Implementing Strategies and Action Plans

"We can't solve problems using the same kind of thinking we used when we created them."

~ Albert Einstein

IN ORDER TO SUCCESSFULLY IMPLEMENT, MANAGE, AND monitor the results of your Strategic Action Plan, you must schedule monthly reviews, quarterly reviews, and annual reviews (see chapter 10). These formal reviews are aimed at determining whether you, your managers, and your employees are on course and moving steadily toward the stated business objectives and strategies.

If you are not on course to meet your business objectives, you need to know sooner rather than later—so that you can rectify the lack of progress.

When holding these review sessions, be sure to first focus on the **positive results**. I repeat: start by reviewing wins, not discussing goals that weren't met or areas where managers and employees fell short. Beginning the review session on a positive note will set a constructive tone and team members will be open to accepting suggestions for change and improvement as the meeting progresses.

Begin each review session with a brief overview of company conditions and financial information; focusing on positive news, announcements, and employee observations and contributions regarding current customers and prospects.

During each meeting you will also consider the data in the monthly reports: financial, sales, and customer service.

Sometimes you might experience a lackluster month or weak quarter; especially during an economic downturn or if there is a lag between product discontinuation and new production and distribution ramp-up. During these times, you might need to take a hard look before you can find a morsel or two of good news—but do look because it is there. Avoid gloom and doom.

Praise fosters positive results!

Next, review the strategies and goals listed in the Strategic Action Plan. Ask the managers and employees assigned to each project to report their results for the month ending. What positive results materialized from their efforts? Were there any negative consequences?

Ask questions.

And ask more questions.

Then listen.

And, take notes.

Evaluate what is working and why it works. Positive outcomes should be encouraged and praised. As the owner, it is your job to laud employees when merited. It motivates them to continue to strive for positive results.

Avoid zeroing in on the negative. Some owners focus immediately on what went wrong because they believe if you fix what does not work, the problem disappears.

But does it really? Maybe; maybe not. Sometimes new issues crop up as a direct result of actions taken. Explore these issues. Most likely, there are answers you can use in them.

Also, by initially focusing on problem areas, strategies that are delivering the results you want sometimes get just a passing glance or entirely overlooked. There are lessons to learn, not just in failure but in areas where there is success.

Other important details to remember for these monthly, quarterly, and annual review sessions:

Never allow criticism of *anyone's* input.

You want everyone on the team to be open to suggestions and share their ideas for improvement to a process or product when problems surface. Criticism by you or other people present at the meeting will not achieve this. The purpose of these meetings is to review and then strategize and plan on how to improve any areas that need it.

Encourage team participation.

Remind managers and employees that when they achieve individual success, it helps the team and the company to achieve its benchmarks—which is beneficial to everyone. Helping each other achieve individually assigned tasks will enable the company at large to achieve its more universal benchmarks for success. This is a team-building process.

Team members should leave these meetings knowing the strategies and tasks they successfully completed and have ideas on how to better complete those that need improvement.

Any serious failure by a manager or employee to produce expected results over a protracted period of time should be individually dealt with by the owner, *in private*.

Using the above approach leaves no room for excuses. By having team members report individually on their assigned tasks, excuses for low performance vaporize. Employees can't point fingers at one another and say, "Hey, Sam was supposed to work on that" or "Sally didn't fix it, so I couldn't do my part."

These meetings offer wonderful opportunities for members to announce breaking news about market developments, and address specific problems that need attention. It is also a great time to tweak the Strategic Action Plan to accommodate ideas that surface during the meeting, ideas that perhaps open a gateway to new markets, prospects, products, and services—but only with your approval, of course.

When I consult with entrepreneurs, I always ask them: Do you have regular Strategic Action Plan review meetings? What do your monthly and quarterly reviews entail? What do you discuss? Who do you include in these meetings?

Answers are revealing.

I've learned that many small business owners review monthly financial reports at the end of the month *following* the month in question, which does not offer timely data. I realize entrepreneurs usually hire outside accountants to prepare financial statements, and because completion of these reports is typically two to five weeks after the fact, valuable time has been lost if there is a problem. Sure, you'll breathe a sigh of relief if you see a profitable month, but if you've lost money, a month or more has passed—and during that time you could have performed a critical review, taken action, and stopped additional financial bleeding.

To avoid this, I required my accountants to provide me with monthly financial **operations** reports that were completed by the *tenth day of each following month*. Impossible, you say? No. I needed the reports sooner, so we took initiative and devised a Strategic Action Plan to accomplish the production of our financial operations statements by the tenth day of the month following the month of interest—and we did it each and every month!

Remember, the accountant and bookkeeper work for you. The managers work for you. You get to decide what data you need and when you want it.

You decide what information you want and when you need it. Accept no excuses from your staff or professional outside consultants.

It is worth repeating: *good business decisions are rooted in facts*. You need reliable information delivered in a timely manner so you can make sound decisions and conduct middle-of-the-month reviews based on the previous month's information. There is no logical reason to depend on data that is a month or more old. Computers and accounting software make it possible for current and "real time" reporting.

Profit-and-Loss Statements

Profit-and-loss scorekeeping focuses on the effects/results of actions—*it does not address causes*. To make the right decisions, you need to learn the causes that are delivering bad results (operations financials). To better evaluate monthly and quarterly strategies you need to call the Strategic Action Plan team together and conduct a thorough review to learn which actions worked and which failed. Then discuss as a group how the team can turn things around in the areas where results and expectations measurably diverged in a negative direction.

Without regular reviews, failure is allowed to persist and managers are allowed to fail.

You gave specific assignments to key people on your team. Your goal: positive and profitable results. What if targets are missed and you don't expose them during review meetings? What message are you sending to employees? Do you want them to think it is okay to not meet assigned goals? Or that no one will be held accountable? That jobs are safe regardless of performance? Is that the message you want to send?

What you make a priority, you will accomplish. When you make monthly, quarterly, and annual review meetings a priority, I assure you, great and positive changes lie ahead.

On the following page, you will find the Strategic Action Plan report form I used. It brings together all of the elements of the Strategic Action Plan and acts as a magnifying glass during the review meetings. The information on this form will help you and the team focus on what is important.

Use the form to extract and report on results-based information; for example, from your financial, personnel, training, sales and marketing, and customer service reports.

I also used this form as the outline and agenda for our review meetings.

> **NOTE:** All of the forms in this book can be downloaded and printed in an 8.5-x-11-inch size by using this link:
> **www.growyourbusiness123.com/downloads.html**

Next: How to perform the annual Strategic Action Plan review.

Strategic Action Plan Results

Company: _____ Date: _____ Business Quarter: _____

Action Plan for Business Year: _____ Results Review for Month of: _____

	Strategy 1	Results Summary
Objective 1		
	Strategy 2	
Objective 2	**Strategy 1**	**Results Summary**
	Strategy 2	

©2016 GYB123

CHAPTER 10

The Annual Review

"In business, the idea of measuring what you are doing, picking the measurements that count, like customer satisfaction and performance ... you thrive on that."

~ Bill Gates

THE ANNUAL STRATEGIC ACTION PLAN REVIEW IS THE SCORE-card of your business activities for the previous twelve months. It differs from the monthly and quarterly reviews just like final grades in high school and college differ from mid-term grades. It holds far more weight and importance.

Once a year, you need to thoroughly review your business with input from key advisers, managers, and employees. Give the Strategic Action Plan team ample notice of the upcoming annual review meeting and require all of the team members to bring their strategic planning documents to the meeting as these will help them focus and follow along as you run the meeting.

I usually held this annual review between the year-end holidays. We closed our business on December 20th (keeping a skeleton staff in the office to field customer visits and phone calls). With business results prepared by the 15th of December for the previous 12 months of operations activities, profitable results information would generate bonuses earned by managers. I distributed bonuses for performance at these meetings—a great motivator for my managers to continue working toward growth in the upcoming year!

Also important: select a location for the Annual Strategic Action Plan Review where there will be no interruptions—and tell team members that all cell phones must be turned OFF.

The annual review meeting is a good time to distribute sales bonuses to managers for positive results!

Annual Review Structure

Use the questions below as a starting point and, if you like, add more of your own. At the meeting, in addition to writing the team's responses on an easel or whiteboard, document what is discussed. Always make copies because you will want to refer to this information later in the year during the quarterly reviews.

Questions you must ask:

1. What strategies worked this past year?

2. Which products and services had the best sales results?

3. Which products and services had the highest sales income?

4. Which products and services had the highest gross-profit results?

5. What strategies did not produce increased sales, income, or profit?

6. What strategies reduced expenses? Which did not?

7. Study your customer and client markets. Which areas performed best? Which fell short of set targets? Any surprises? List them.

8. What other strategies worked well? Review all training for new employees, advertising, and customer-service projects you put in place during the past year. What new problems cropped up? Describe them in detail.

9. What opportunities did you and the team discover?

10. Have you identified new products, markets, or services you can offer? List them.

11. Do you see untapped human capital—existing talent you can promote or new talent that should be hired and leveraged to move the company forward? Discuss.

Next, take a break from brainstorming to review your business's mission, purpose, and objectives.

In my experience, I found that reading these items aloud, word by word to the team, helped emphasize the importance of these elements and kept the annual review meeting on target.

These elements are vital to your business's success. They

determine the direction of your Strategic Action Planning efforts.

Agenda for the Annual Review Meeting

These are the steps I followed for the annual reviews. I suggest you do the same.

STEP 1

Read your MISSION Statement, which should never change.

STEP 2

Read your PURPOSE. Although I never found a need to change my purpose statements once they were inked, I know some businesses do alter theirs; sometimes because a market change dictated a need or ownership changed and the direction of the business was subsequently altered.

STEP 3

Read your OBJECTIVES. Test each one. Are you meeting your Strategic Business Plan objectives? If the answer is yes, then no changes are required; but if you are dealing with new problems and opportunities, or falling short of targets in some areas, change will be necessary.

STEP 4

Review and evaluate *each* company objective independently to determine if you are achieving that objective. On target?

Are you achieving the "performance standards" for each business function?

If yes, then the objective remains valid and it is okay to move onto the next item. Not on target? Then ask why and discuss ways the team can make it work. If there are no plausible solutions, amend the performance standard or consider scrapping that particular objective.

STEP 5

The team will examine and discuss any P's & O's (problems and opportunities) exposed during the meeting. After that, review your Spy Book information (see chapter 5); and finally discuss defensive strategies you can use to solve any problems and the methods you will use to exploit new opportunities.

To discuss this successfully, you will need access to year-end business operations reports (see the list on page 116). It is the only way to perform a quality annual review.

Traditional reporting often fails to tell the whole story—the good, the bad, and the ugly.

Sometimes the bad news gets buried in the fluff, but when the whole team is part of the review process and the right data is available, failings and successes become obvious and it is easier to expose and deal with them.

Following is a list of the management reports I required in the course of doing business. I had them in-hand for monthly meetings, quarterly reviews, and always for the critical annual review meeting.

Since everything is computerized, you should insist on this information by the tenth of each month for the previous month.

▲ **Sales Reports** (prepared by bookkeeper/administrative assistant)

▲ **Customer Service Reports** (prepared by the adminstration manager and selected key employees)

▲ **Company Project Reports for each product line and market segment** (prepared by each project manager and/or key employees)

▲ **Manufacturing Production Reports** (If you manufacture a product) focusing on timlieness and quality percentage.

▲ **Departmental Operating Statements for income, sales costs, gross profit, expenses, and net-profit results** (Be sure to deduct debt reduction and income tax from net profit in order to communicate the true picture of net profit. Prepared by bookkeeper but withhold the financial balance sheet, which should remain confidential to you, the owner)

Entrepreneurs oftentimes allow managers, accountants, and bookkeepers to determine when their reports will be produced and delivered. Management decisions and Strategic Action Plans are then held hostage to someone else's timetable. In today's fast-changing market, lack of timely information can cripple a small business and prevent you from making good decisions. You won't make profits with old data!

As they say, the devil is in the details. In these reports, you will find what works and what does not. Find the devils and toss them out before they rob you of profits.

When my managers generated reports on schedule, *by the fifth day of the month for the previous month closed*, it was a simple task to group the prior month's or quarter's data together. Not difficult when using a computer.

It is no different with accounting and bookkeeping. Yes, you will hear excuses. My accounting staff often complained, "We can't give you the reports you need until we make adjustments for depreciation, state and federal taxes, and close the books," and on and on. For a time, I accepted their answers, but one day I became enlightened and discovered the morsels I needed and realized I didn't have to wait for a formal final report. What I wanted was basic operations management information—a lower level of detail than what bookkeepers and accountants have to prepare for final IRS reports when a new fiscal year rolls around—but it was accurate information.

Although they complained, I knew their efforts weren't wasted. The same material they generated for me would eventually be used to close the books—after they dotted every "i," corrected accounting errors, and added every column. We are creatures of habit and I broke up their routine. So, they objected to the interruption of *their* process to pull base operational information reports for *my* strategic planning meetings.

Remember: as the owner, you are in control.

You can force compliance by instructing staff to produce the timely reports you and your planning team need for strategizing. Accept no excuses for not providing the reports when you want them.

STEP 6

Review the Strategic Action Plan for the past fiscal year. Read each strategy and consider its effectiveness. Did it work? Why or why not? Record answers from the team and analyze what to do going forward—continue as planned? Amend the strategy? Or abort the strategy altogether?

This is called *brainstorming*. When team members use their imaginations and openly share their thoughts and ideas.

Imagination: the act of forming a mental image of something not present to the senses; in short, a mental image or creation of the mind.

Don't criticize the input offered either, because doing so will choke creativity; and you want innovative ideas brought to light. You want your Strategic Action Plan to succeed! And as always, take notes of the responses you receive from team members and offer praise and congratulations where earned.

Later, in the quiet of your private office, reflect on the information generated at the annual review meeting and finalize your decisions. Then, distribute the Strategic Action Plan for the current year within a week to the team.

Congratulations!
You have just completed an annual review!

At this point, you have completed a full cycle of Strategic Business Planning for your company. This is a repeatable process that must be ongoing if you are serious about wanting ever-increasing sales, income, and profit.

I hope you enjoyed the journey as much as I have enjoyed sharing it with you.

CONCLUSION

I USE THE WORDS *JOURNEY* AND *DESTINATION* THROUGHOUT this book. Do you know the difference between the two?

A *destination* is a place someone is going. I use it to describe the annual, short-term goals of a Strategic Business Plan.

A *journey* is the act of moving from one place to another. In this book it represents the trip an entrepreneur takes— from startup through Phases 1 and 2, and into the future, where you can achieve your long-range goals of expansion.

As I reflect on my business journey, I realize that the values I adopted early on had a direct impact on the positive results I achieved. Values that stayed with me, motivated me, and ultimately helped lead to many business (and personal) successes.

Most successful entrepreneurs discover specific business values as they progress in life and grow their businesses— and the smart entrepreneurs will both write them down and commit the values to memory. There are many values I attribute to my success; the three most important ones are:

Planning

Commitment

Persistence

To these values I credit my forty-five years of successful business operation. These words hung framed on a wall in my office, serving as a constant reminder of what to do and what not to do.

They were not easily visible to visitors and managers, only to me, *for my benefit*, something to glance at and reflect on before answering the phone or meeting with visitors throughout the day.

You can learn more about these values in Appendix A. They are intended as positive catalysts for change and "thought helpers"—aids for the journey you are taking on the road to ever-increasing sales, income, and profit.

I strongly believe good values are critical to personal and business success. I also hung these values on the living room walls of my mind, to influence my decision-making and to crowd out any negative influences that might deter me in my journey to successful results.

Take a look around. We live in a competitive world. And now, more than ever, the United States needs you and your small business to succeed.

There are approximately 30 million unemployed or under-employed Americans in the country today, and they will not find that big government, big education, big finance, or big business are in a position to help them. Most assistance for the unemployed and underemployed will come from the small business sector which "is our nation's engine of economic growth, responsible for 75% of all net new jobs."[1] It contributes "between 65% and 80% of all new jobs in the U.S. annually, and has done so throughout the past several decades."[2]

Values are what you believe in, and what you believe

---

1. Wolk, M. "Small Business Having a Big Impact on Jobs." published online at http://www.msnbc.msn.com/id/4142727/ns/business- small business/ [cited February 3, 2011].
2. Office of Advocacy, U.S. Small Business Administration inquiry on October 26, 2010

powers you forward in your quest for success. The values I write about in Appendix A, when embraced, can help make your journey easier, faster, and more successful.

Every business startup is powered by entrepreneurs convinced their business idea is going to succeed. They risk capital—their own and sometimes that of family, friends, financial institutions, and even angel investors—to make what starts as a dream materialize and prosper—but only a few succeed. Why? Primarily it is poor initial and ongoing strategic business planning that pulls them down, followed by an inability to commit themselves to the dream—results take work, *hard* work. And you might not see big results right away.

Essential to entrepreneurial success is a commitment to Strategic Business Planning.

Without continual and ongoing strategic planning, it gets too easy to walk away when results aren't quick or visible. A good hold on all three—planning, commitment, and perseverance—is a great start, but letting just one topple can bring the whole business to a screeching halt. That is why proper strategic planning is crucial to success.

Remember, 80 percent of all business startups fail in the first year, and that same percentage again for those who make it to the one- to three-year survival period before reaching the five-year (I think we made it!) mark.

Who reaches (and stays) in the winner's circle?

Entrepreneurs who employ and are committed to Strategic Business Plans.

Entrepreneurs who know how to persevere despite encountering obstacles.

If Thomas Edison hadn't been such an entrepreneur, we might all still be sitting in the dark.

Are you impassioned enough to commit to making your company succeed? Your purchase of this book indicates to me that you are.

Still, this book is not enough. You must manage your time well and separate the wheat from the chaff. Do what needs doing first and let the less important take a back-seat—otherwise you could find yourself telling friends over coffee, "I had a small business," when what you really want to do is shout, "I am the proud owner of a successful small business!"

Yes, life gets in the way, and sometimes following through on strategies and actions isn't easy. Struggles between you, family, and friends are sure to erupt. Today it takes a 24/7 commitment to avoid business setbacks or impending disasters, and to stay ahead of the competition—but keep your eye on the prize: a successful business that rewards you with job satisfaction, wealth, and independence.

I wish you good luck—although I'm sure you know by now success is not rooted in a lucky streak, like a spin at the roulette wheel in Vegas. In fact, I don't discuss luck in the context of business success anywhere in the book because luck plays no part. Luck is simply when preparedness meets opportunity. You prepare by your willingness to work hard and sacrifice. Then opportunities present themselves and you become "lucky"—but none of it happens without Strategic Business Planning and hard work.

ACKNOWLEDGMENTS

THE CONTENTS OF THIS BOOK DRAW UPON MY BUSINESS experiences, plus the talents, expertise, and know-how others shared with me over a business career that spanned more than four decades. I want to thank those individuals who offered me insight, encouragement, and support along the way.

DONALD C. WERME, ASM, friend and business colleague. A successful small business owner and executive in the field of corporate self-insured health insurance benefits, stop-loss reinsurance, and health claims data management.

WILLIAM F. HAMILTON, ASM, friend and business associate, who after a successful career as an executive at several of my companies, founded a successful health insurance managing general agency in Kalamazoo, Michigan.

JUDITH A. RODOCKER, a long-time business associate and friend. She is truly one of the most talented business administration senior executives I have had the pleasure of working with.

STEVEN P. STUCKY, CLU, business colleague, friend, adviser, and able fishing partner for over thirty-six years. A highly successful insurance company executive and small business owner, he is also a nationally recognized leader in the development of smaller corporation stop-loss reinsurance for health insurance employee benefits and health insurance claims administration and management.

DEAN S. LEWIS, Esq., friend, legal counselor, and thoughtful adviser on a multitude of business issues. I thank him for his ever-present support throughout the continuum of my business ventures.

WILLIAM R. COLE, retired president and CEO of First of America Bancorp-Michigan. He has been a friend for years. As a practicing loan officer in the 1970s and 1980s, he belonged to the "old school of lenders"—those who (after due diligence, of course) believed that a person's word was their bond. He was a trusted adviser and confidante on matters of banking and finance.

EVAN P. KOKALES, MD, dear friend and avid supporter of improving the human condition. A medical director/manager with a brilliant mind and ample knowledge of the broader issues surrounding health, healthcare delivery, and the competing forces between participants.

HARRY H. HINEMAN, ASA, Chief Actuary (retired) of Indiana Blue Cross, an actuarial giant in the field of healthcare claims expenses, claims forecasting, and healthcare financing. He regularly offered a steady hand and good advice while directing me toward business solvency and operating profits.

JAMES F. SCARPONE, CPA, CVA, CFA, friend and adviser with an incredible ability to merge financial accounting, tax responsibilities, and "good old business sense" into a powerful source of assistance. He showed me how to successfully manage the financial growth of a Phase 2 small business.

PATRICIA H. SICILANO, RHU, a successful, high-energy sales and marketing executive with a flair for making "good things happen," many for my benefit, earning her my special praise.

THEA PREATER LAPHAM, author, prolific writer, and self-publishing consultant. She was a highly energetic promoter of small business and in 2002, provided me with the inspiration to write. I believe, though I don't fully understand it, that her spirit has been urging me to fulfill the dream of writing this book.

MARY JO ZAZUETA, editor, publishing guide, entrepreneur, and principle at To The Point Solutions, whom I met in 2014. Her professional guidance helped me focus my message to entrepreneurs and made this book possible.

CHRIS NYE, website designer and social media consultant.

Thank you all for joining in my journey.

READY FOR FRAMING AND HANGING

Inspirational words are timeless and priceless. If you would like enlarged prints of the quotes in Appendix A to frame and hang in your office, please visit the link below.

www.growyourbusiness123.com/downloads.html

Quotes to Guide and Inspire

LEADERS go places, but not alone.

They take others with them. Their ability to set up situations in which other people are willing to follow is a precious skill. This skill is made up of thoughtfulness and consideration of others and a multitude of other traits. But fundamentally, a leader is one who has a plan. One who leads, one who heads toward a goal with purpose.

Leaders have the enthusiasm to keep moving forward in such a way that others GO with them.

AUTHOR UNKNOWN

"Whatever you can do or dream you can, begin it. Boldness has genius, power, and magic in it."

JOHANN WOLFGANG VON GOETHE

"Can-do is a hearty soul!"

EMMA JANE CUMMINGS
1870-1957 (MY GRANDMOTHER)

Commitment

Until one is committed there is hesitancy, the chance to draw back, always ineffectiveness.

Concerning all the acts of initiative (and reason), there is one elementary truth, the ignorance of which kills countless ideas and splendid plans, that the moment one definitely commits oneself, then providence moves too. All sorts of things occur to help one that would never otherwise have occurred. A whole stream of events issues from the decision, raising in one's favor all manner of unforeseen incidents and meetings and material assistance, which no man could have dreamt would have come his (or her) way.

W. H. Murray

Persistence

Nothing in the world can take the place of persistence.

Talent will not, nothing is more common than unsuccessful men with talent.

Genius will not, the world is full of educated derelicts.

Persistence and determination alone are omnipotent.

The slogan "press on" has solved and always will solve the problems of the human race.

Calvin Coolidge

In a race—everyone runs

but only ONE person wins first prize.
So run your race to win.

1 Corinthians 9:24

The new idea either finds a champion or dies …

No ordinary involvement with a new idea provides the energy required to cope with the indifference and resistance that major technological (or process) change provokes …

Champions of new inventions (ideas) display persistence and courage of heroic quality.

EDWARD SCHON

If

If you can dream and not make dreams your master;
If you can think—and not make thoughts your aim,
If you can meet with triumph and disaster
And treat those two imposters just the same;

If you can bear to hear the truth you've spoken
Twisted by knaves to make a trap for fools,
Or watch the things you gave your life to, broken,
And stoop and build 'em up with worn-out tools;

If you can fill the unforgiving minute
With sixty seconds worth of distance run:
Yours is the earth and everything that's in it,
And—which is more a [winner] you will be!

If there is something in life you want and don't get,
Either you did not want it bad enough or tried to bargain over the price.

RUDYARD KIPLING

What kind of pictures do you hang
on the living room walls of your mind?
Are they success pictures, or are they failure pictures?

Think positively, you win.

Think negatively, you lose.

RICHARD B. SANFORD

"A day of worry is more exhausting than a week of work."
DOROTHY CARNEGIE,
HOW TO STOP WORRYING AND START LIVING

"Prestige is running your own business."
MATT ROUS

READY FOR FRAMING AND HANGING

If you would like a larger, multi-colored copy of **Sanford's Pyramid of Business Success** to hang in your office, please visit the link below.

www.growyourbusiness123.com/downloads.html

An Entrepreneur's Toolbox

SANFORD'S PYRAMID OF BUSINESS SUCCESS

The management process for
Simplified Strategic Business Planning.

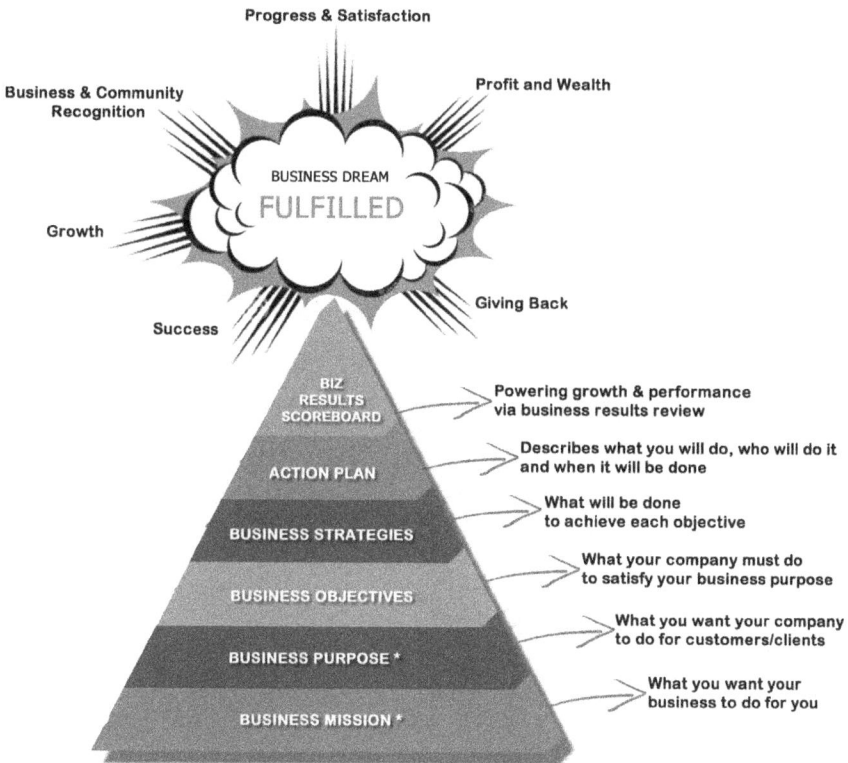

Progress & Satisfaction

Business & Community Recognition

Profit and Wealth

BUSINESS DREAM
FULFILLED

Growth

Giving Back

Success

BIZ RESULTS SCOREBOARD — Powering growth & performance via business results review

ACTION PLAN — Describes what you will do, who will do it and when it will be done

BUSINESS STRATEGIES — What will be done to achieve each objective

BUSINESS OBJECTIVES — What your company must do to satisfy your business purpose

BUSINESS PURPOSE * — What you want your company to do for customers/clients

BUSINESS MISSION * — What you want your business to do for you

* The Foundation of Every Business

PERSONAL TOOLS

Thinking
(The ability to consider and ponder)

Imagination
(The ability to dream of change and new ideas)

Vision
(The ability to form vivid mental images of the future)

Oral Communication
(The ability to clearly express your thoughts verbally)

Written Communication
(The ability to clearly express yourself in writing)

COMMON TOOLS

Dictionary

Thesaurus

Encyclopedia and other research and reference materials *(both online and in print)*

GLOSSARY

Action Plan: The process and steps that are needed to achieve particular goals over a given period of time.

Mission: What a business does for the entrepreneur/owner.

Objectives: A goal based on facts rather than opinions or feelings.

Phase 1 small business: A small business that has survived the first-year start-up phase and is generating profitable results going forward. Most of these businesses will remain small and many become profitable. Many are family owned and controlled, and have few employees.

Phase 2 small business: A small business that has survived both the start-up and Phase 1 period of business growth, which encompasses the first- to third-year "frequent failure" segment of time when a company's ability to survive in the marketplace is truly tested. Typically at this phase the entrepreneurial owner has a desire and passion to really expand and grow the business which means adding to the workforce (employees) and enlisting the aid of managers to help train and direct activities in pursuit of increased sales, income, and profit.

Purpose: What a business does for customers/clients.

Results reviews: A retrospective view or survey of business results.

Startup: A new small business with an entrepreneurial owner or owners.

Strategy: A logical plan or method for achieving a goal or objective.

BIBLIOGRAPHY

Barnes & Noble Inc., "1998 Annual Report" Published online athttp://www.barnesandnobleinc.com/for_investors/annual_reports/bnannual98.pdf [cited January 31, 2011].

Barnes & Noble Inc., "2008 Annual Report" Published online at http://www.barnesandnobleinc.com/for_investors/annual_reports/bnannual08.pdf [cited January 31, 2011].

Irwin Financial Corporation, "2004 Annual Report." Published online at http://www.annualreports.com/HostedData/AnnualReports/PDFArchive/ifc2004.pdf [cited February 5, 2011]

McConkey, D. "How to Manage By Results." New York: American Management Association, 1987.

Schumpeter, J.A. Capitalism, *Socialism and Democracy*, 3rd ed. New York: Harper & Row, 1950.

Stryker Corporation, "Welcome to Stryker" Published online at http://www.stryker.com/en- us/index.htm. [cited January 31, 2011].

Wolk, M. "Small Business Having a Big Impact on Jobs." Published online at http:///www.msnbc.msn.com/id/4142727/ns/business-small_business/ [cited February 3, 2011].

ABOUT THE AUTHOR

RICHARD B. (Dick) SANFORD began his life as an entrepreneur in 1945 at the age of fourteen, when a change in family circumstances required that he live alone and provide for most of his living expenses. He started with a newspaper route. When that income proved insufficient, he decided to increase his work hours and added an additional set of deliveries. It wasn't long before the budding entrepreneur was managing both a big city morning paper delivery and two afternoon local prints.

Delivering newspapers taught Sanford valuable business lessons no MBA program could. He learned business "street smarts" firsthand. He saw that to succeed in business it wasn't enough to show up for work on time. There was more. He needed to cultivate a loyal customer base and grow his business through word of mouth—which all hinged on providing excellent customer service. He also mastered the "art of the deal," as he perfected handling late-paying and non-paying customers.

Still a youth, but expected to labor like an adult, Sanford developed a keen understanding of time's value and how to plan a day's work. Proper planning was key if he was to both attend school—and pass—while working almost fulltime.

Because work was all he knew, Sanford explains, "At the time, it didn't seem to be too much of a task. Nothing seems impossible when you are young. Even dreams seem reachable."

Sanford always remembered his Grandmother Emma's wise words: "Can-do is a hearty soul." In fact, it is how he lives. His early work experiences shaped the vision and reality of the eleven companies he later founded.

You can learn more about the author by visiting www.growyourbusiness123.com.

INDEX

PASS IT ON

Perhaps you have friends and business associates who are interested in expanding their businesses, people who can benefit from reading *Growing Your Business 1, 2,* 3 and learning how to formulate a Strategic Business Plan. Please direct them to Amazon where they can order a copy of this book.

Thank you for your help in spreading the word on how to create ever-increasing sales, income, and profit in the world of small business.

Every business success is important (especially an entrepreneurial one). If you wish to share how a Strategic Business Plan helped your business grow, please contact me at:

sanford@growyourbusiness123.com

www.ingramcontent.com/pod-product-compliance
Lightning Source LLC
Chambersburg PA
CBHW062010200326
41519CB00017B/4746

9 780692 619872